JESSE

JESSE

a spiritual autobiography

by JESSE OWENS
with Paul Neimark

LOGOS INTERNATIONAL Plainfield, New Jersey

Epigraphs taken from *Excelsior* by Henry Wadsworth Longfellow.

JESSE
Copyright © 1978 by Jesse Owens, Paul Neimark
All rights reserved
Printed in the United States of America
Library of Congress Catalog Card Number: 78-59857
International Standard Book Number: 0-88270-314-5
Logos International, Plainfield, New Jersey 07060

Jesse Owens dedicates this book to:

Two unmatchable teammates:
My wife of almost fifty years, Ruth,
And the Nazi
Who fought Hitler with me,
Luz Long;

Three unique leaders:
My father,
My mother,
And Charles Riley.

But, most, and most humbly,
To The Great Referee.

JESSE

The shades of night
were falling fast. . . .

CHAPTER ONE

The first prayer I ever made saved my life though I didn't know I was praying, and afterward I never remembered a word I said.

But the fear and the fever which led up to it—and the blood—are still burned in my mind.

I first noticed the bump the morning after my fifth birthday. Birthdays were something you always remembered where I spent the early years of my life, because it was one of the thirteen times a year my mother served meat for our daily meal. Once for each of our ten birthdays, Easter, Christmas and, some years, the Fourth of July. Before my next birthday, though, we would be eating meat two times less because two of the children would die that year, as two others had died at birth before them. And as the bump on my chest grew in as well as out, making it harder and harder for me to breathe with every sunset, it seemed more and more with each passing day that five birthdays were all I would ever have.

There was no doctor to be called. Decatur was the nearest town of size, and they didn't have one. Sure, there was one in Birmingham, seventy-five miles away. But it really wouldn't have mattered if the finest surgeon in the world had been spending the night with our next-door neighbors, the Stepparts, a mile down. We didn't have a cent. Not a cent. Sharecropping was a kind name for my father's work.

The name of our town was Oakville, but it was more dozens and dozens of farms than a real town. Each farm was worked by a Negro family—and the whole family did work it, from the time you were old enough to walk. Every three or four farms, sometimes as many as a dozen, were owned by one landlord. He rented you your tools, and the "house" you lived in, and even the food you ate (because if you didn't have any money there wasn't any food until harvest time). Then, when you picked the crops, the landlord took the bigger percentage to sell, and gave you your smaller percentage, from which he deducted everything you owed him for what he'd let you use.

What was left we divided into two parts. The first was what we needed to survive through the winter—the food we put aside and stored, and some we sold back to the boss for enough money to buy that rare meat meal, and one good shirt for each of us for church. The second part was profit.

For us—for all our neighbors and, as I was later to

4

learn, for millions and millions of Americans both white and black in the second decade of the twentieth century—not starving was the best you could do. My daddy had begun working for the boss, Mr. Clannon, when he was still almost a boy himself, with only the mule his own father—who'd died of overwork—had left him, and the clothes on his body. Now, thirty years later, he had no more earthly possessions than that mule and the shredded clothes he wore to shield him from the sun.

No, there wasn't money for a doctor.

And the bump kept growing larger.

One night, though sometimes it was hard to hear anything because I was gasping so when I lay down now, I could overhear my parents talking about it. "We've got to do something, Henry," my mother whispered.

"You took one off his leg once, Emma."

"But this one's so big. And near his heart."

"Emma—"

"Don't say it, Henry!"

"I'm going to say it. If the Lord wants him—"

"The Lord doesn't want this child," my mother said, her voice rising above a whisper for the first time. My momma had always called me her "gift child," not only because I was the last born that would carry the Owens name, but because she claimed "he was made when he couldn't have been made by us."

Finally, I was gasping so loud I couldn't even hear their words. I fell asleep out of exhaustion I guess what must have been a couple of hours before sunup. But I also was awakened before the dawn—and this time it wasn't because I could hardly breathe. It was my mother shaking me. There was water boiling in both our kettles at the fireplace. All my brothers and sisters were awake. Momma took a knife, held it in the fire a long time, and then came over to where I was lying. "I'm going to take off the bump now, J.C.," she said.

Once I'd gotten into a fight with the boss's twelve-year-old son because he called my mother a bad name, and he yelled for his older brother and they started to carve their initials on my face before my own brothers got wind of it. And then there was that other bump my mother took off my leg. And the time I wanted to prove I was a man and went out in the fields by myself and got caught in a trap my daddy had set. I thought I knew pain those times, but I didn't. Real pain is when you don't have any choice any more whether to cry or not, and then maybe you don't even cry because it wouldn't help. I always hated to go to sleep at night, but now for the first time in my life I wanted to pass out. Something inside wouldn't let me. All I felt was the knife going deeper, around and around, trying to cut that thing loose, all I saw were the tears running down my father's face, all I heard was my own voice—but like it was somebody else's from far-off—moaning, "Aww, Momma, no. . . ."

Finally, it was over, and I did lapse into unconsciousness. It was dark when I woke up. I never knew if it was the same day. Everyone was still in the house. I could tell from their clothes that they hadn't gone out in the fields. There were only two other times when the whole family hadn't gone out to work the crops. Christmas Day was one. When someone in our house died was the other.

I was only five years old, but I knew I was dying.

I tried to speak, but I actually couldn't get the words out. I didn't have the strength, and my throat wouldn't seem to work. When they saw I was awake, they gathered around me. My mother had gotten it out, she said, all of it. But what she didn't say was that it was too deep, that I was bleeding, and that nothing they could do would stop the bleeding.

They kept trying things, my momma and daddy, and when nothing worked they kept soaking up the blood with crop bags, then with the rags we use for towels, then with some of their own clothing because the blood was coming faster than my mother could wash and dry.

The next day, my father, my brother Sylvester and the others had to go out and work in the fields, but my mother stayed, not even trying to end the bleeding any more, just trying to keep it from getting all over me, and hoping somehow it would stop. But it didn't. At last, even she fell asleep, exhausted, at my side. I tried not to let the blood get onto her, but I could hardly move and sometime later, I looked in horror as I saw the redness crawling under her own blouse like a monster!

Maybe it was seeing that, maybe it was all the blood I had lost, but I was pulled under once again no matter how I tried to fight it. I'm not sure how many times I was awake after that, because none of them were for longer than a minute or two. Each time, my first thought was, *Is the wetness still there? Am I still bleeding?* I always was. It never stopped. And I knew, the way you know on the bottom line, whether you're five or fifty years old, that there wasn't much lifeblood left in me to bleed out.

I think the third night after the cutting was when I heard it. My mother had fallen asleep at my side again, after praying for hours, though it seemed from the tone of her voice that she was praying more for my soul than my life. But what I heard was different. It was fuzzy—because everything was—but I could make out my father's voice, in a hoarse whisper from what seemed like miles away. I lifted myself as much as I could, first on a shoulder and then on an elbow, tried to hear, to see. But it was one of those moonless Alabama September nights and my eyes told me nothing, my ears not enough.

Yet something in me stirred, something I had never felt before. It gave me the strength to actually sit up for the first time, though shaking from weakness. I felt even more blood trickle down from my chest onto my stomach and legs, as I lifted my body up higher. But it made the words come more clearly.

"She'll die—" he was saying. What did it mean? Somehow, I moved closer to where the voice was coming from. He wasn't miles away. He was only outside the front door. Everyone else was asleep.

"Oh, Lord Jesus," he went on. "Please . . . please hear me . . . I know you hears everything . . . but this . . . saving . . . means everything. . . ."

"She'll die if he dies—and if she dies, Lord, we'll all die—all of us—"

I crawled closer to the doorway, inch by inch. The blood was coming in erratic spurts now, and I knew, partly because of a glowing kind of haziness that was taking me over and scaring me deeper than I'd ever been scared, and partly because I just knew, that it was because my body was emptying of blood.

"He's my last boy—J.C.'s the one you gave me last to carry my name—she'll die if you take him from me—she always said he was born special—she said he was made when he couldn't be—"

I felt like I was going to faint again, so I dug my nails, every nail of both hands, into the wood of the floor like it was the dirt in the fields outside, and I hung on, pulled myself toward the open doorway, until I could make out the figure of my father.

"Please don't take him from me, Lord—I'll do anything—the hardest thing—anything to pay you back—J.C.!"

My father turned to me—we were both kneeling, he in prayer and me because I couldn't stand—and instantly reached out to take me in his arms and carry me back inside. But when his hand touched me, touched the red wet layer of cloth above my heart, he stopped. There was still no moon, it was one of the darkest nights I can remember. But somehow I could see his eyes looking into mine. "Pray, J.C.," he told me. "Pray, James Cleveland."

I'd prayed in church, of course, and heard my family

pray. But this was different. I'd never prayed on my own. For the first time in days, I heard myself speak: "What should I say, Daddy?"

I don't know what he answered.

I don't know what I said. I don't know how long we knelt there together, side by side.

I only know I prayed.

And I know, too, that when he did lift me in his arms to carry me back into the house, the bleeding had stopped.

As through a . . . village passed. . . .

CHAPTER TWO

And the bleeding never started again.

The next day, I was sitting up easily, eating like our mule by dinner time. The day after that, I was walking around. By the weekend, I was out in the fields again, helping.

But it took more than me and all my brothers and sisters helping my father in the fields for us to survive. We all knew my being alive was because of the power of prayer. Yet how could you pray for more money from the boss? The harvest was good, but after Mr. Clannon added up everything, it came out so that we would hardly have enough to get us through the winter. And even my daddy's one mule was in danger now.

"If you don't come up with some money between now and Christmas," the boss told my father, "I'll have to take the mule and sell him at market."

"But where else am I gonna come up with anythin' 'cept from the land?"

There was no way. My father had no skills—how could he have any? He was like millions of other black men after the turn of the century, whose fathers or grandfathers had been born slaves. He didn't know anything but sharecropping, and were a million Negroes supposed to pray for history to go back two hundred years so that things wouldn't be this way, or for all the bosses like Mr. Clannon to suddenly get goodhearted?

As October became November and turned into December, our home became quieter. The one thing we'd always looked forward to was Christmas, no matter how far away it was. There'd been a couple of Christmases when it seemed like there was no way we'd have meat, but somehow my momma always made that kind of miracle happen and there it was, on the table, when you woke up Christmas morning. And, though there were no gifts we could give each other, my daddy or one of my brothers always found some tree miles away somewhere on wild land, and we put maybe a little piece of bright string we'd saved and some silver wrapping one of my sisters found in the boss's throwaway and even our socks that we were going to wear later to church, to decorate it. My brother, Quincy, and I were the youngest boys, and even if we'd been fighting, we stayed close the night before waiting for that tree to appear in the familiar southeast corner of the room. But it didn't this time.

The next morning, we both awoke early, hoping

somehow maybe to see the tree then, and put what we had on it. But the corner of the room was still empty. And there was no smell—because even though you smelled it only a couple of times a year, you could never forget it—of meat in the fireplace.

The nine-mile walk to church that morning was a long one, yet the journey home was even longer. I usually looked forward to church because it was a chance to see boys my own age, and the singing made everybody happy. And I liked it, too, because my parents always seemed to come back lifted up, my father talking about how this year we were going to start to save, get ahead for the first time, my mother saying how it might not be too long before we'd have meat once a week, and maybe some of us would even go to the high school thirty miles away, and not have to end up sharecropping the land. And sometimes all the rest of us would talk about our dreams, like what we wanted if the day ever came when we could get Christmas presents for each other, and what we would like to be when we grew up. The girls, of course, didn't dare to dream that they could be anything, and only hoped they'd get married to men where they didn't have to slave as hard as my mother. My brother, Prentice, said he'd like to own a small piece of land someday, actually buy it from the boss, so no one could tell him what to do. My brother, Quincy, said he'd like to get to the big city somehow, and keep up some building there, wash it down with lye soap like my mother used to wash the walls and floor of our house. Each time we walked home from church, every one of them would say the same thing, while all the rest listened like they were hearing it for the first time. Though, when it came my turn finally, instead of everyone being real quiet, they would start smiling, some even laughing. For my dream was something I heard about from the boss's son when we weren't fighting one day. He told me how when he grew up, Mr. Clannon was going to put him on a train, and he was going to sleep on that train for a whole night until the next day it stopped at some place more than a state away, because in that place there was a special school where you could become anything in the world that you wanted to become!

It was called a *kolledge*.

So all I ever said, when it came my turn was, "I wanta go to *kolledge!*"

And then everyone would have a big laugh on me, sometimes for five minutes. And when it had quieted down, my mother would grab me gently by the ear and pull me to her and hug me and shake her head and say, "James Cleveland Owens—where in this world do you get your idees? You are the one!"

"The crazy one," my father would say. And then everyone would start laughing again.

But this morning, as we walked home from church, no one talked. And no one laughed. Once we were inside the house, it was no different. Sunday, in the months after harvest and before planting, was my father's day of rest and he would spend it talking to my mother, or whittling, or playing some games with the rest of us when he wasn't too tired. My mother would spend most of the time working, cleaning the house and getting our clothes washed to go out in the fields again, but she always had a little time to tell us a story or two about her own kin, and about her own granddaddy in particular, and the time he talked back to the man who owned him.

Yet this Christmas Day, she had no stories and my father only sat in the wooden chair he'd made, his pipe in his mouth, staring off into space. The fire in the pipe had gone out, but he didn't light it again.

"You want to play, Sylvester?" I asked my brother.

He shook his head. "I don't feel like it today, J.C."

I asked my other brothers and sisters, but no one was in the mood. I got my little sister to play hide-and-seek for a while, but I was never much good at the hide part, and we stopped after about ten minutes. When I came back into the house, my mother and father weren't there. "Where's momma? Where's daddy?"

"They out in the fields," Sylvester said.

"What are they doin' out there on Sunday winter?"

"They talkin', J.C.," Sylvester said. "You stay right here until they through."

I waited until Sylvester went off to fix one of his tools, and silently left the house. I was going to get to play hide-and-seek after all, and the part I liked best—seeking!

My daddy's "share" was big, near forty acres.

And he and my momma must have really wanted to talk, because they weren't anywhere I could see. I kept circling and circling, making sure I didn't miss a corner, till I was way at the other end, the line that divided where my daddy worked from Mr. Clannon's personal land. But they were nowhere to be found.

There was only one place left. It was a rocky place, too rocky to ever be worked, though the boss counted it every year and took it off my father's share. It was between the north border of our land, and Joe Steppart's. All Joe's wife's babies were born dead, and he had to work his land alone. His share wasn't as big as ours, but he did it all by himself, and I never saw a man so thin. I was skinny and sickly, but nothing like Joe Steppart, who was a grown man. I hated to even look at him. He seemed to get thinner every year.

I raced to the rocky place as fast as I could go. I always loved running. I wasn't very good at it, but I loved it because it was something you could do all by yourself, all under your own power. You could go in any direction, fast or slow as you wanted, fighting the wind if you felt like it, seeking out new sights just on the strength of your feet and the courage of your lungs.

I heard them before I saw them. They were talking loud, because they figured no one was anywhere near. I hunkered down behind this strange shaped boulder and listened. I think it was the only time I heard my father raise his voice to my mother.

"Emma, you're talking like J.C.! Crazy!"

"It's crazy to go on like this, Henry!"

"We've got no choice."

"Folks have done it."

"Who?"

"You heard about it, same as I have. Folks have done it!"

"And never been heard from again!"

"Why should they? Why should they come back?" My mother's voice softened for a minute. "And how could they ever write, Henry? How many colored people knows how to write? Do you think if you stay working for the boss here that any of your own young-uns will ever learn how to put words on paper? They'll make their mark, an X, just like you have to do."

My father didn't answer for a minute. Finally, he did. His voice was even softer than my mother's, and sad. "We'd never make it, Emma. We'd starve. First J.C. and the little one, then the others and then you and me. We'd starve in a week. We'd never get there."

My mother raised her voice again. "We're nearly starving here."

"Nearly."

Neither one of them said anything for the longest time. I was afraid they'd heard me breathing, from all the running. Then my father spoke again. This time his voice was different, not shouting, not soft. "It can't be done, Emma. So we're not going to do it. That's my final word."

What *were* they talking about?

I didn't have time to try and figure it, because suddenly someone came running from across the way. Without thinking, I just stood right up, and my mother and daddy saw me. I never could hide for very long.

"J.C.! What you doin' here?" my mother exclaimed.

"Get on back to the house as fast as you can go!" my father shouted.

I'd only gotten one licking in my life from my daddy—the time I carved up some soap to look like an onion and my mother put it in the Sunday stew and the house was full of bubbles for hours and no one ate that day—and I sure didn't want another. So I lit out, but not quite as fast as I could go, because I wanted to see who was coming. It was Jim Turner, who owned a share on the other side of the Stepparts. "Henry! Emma!" I heard him shout. "I was comin' to tell ya! It's turrible—*turrible*! Joe Steppart and his missus was just found! They both hung themselves!"

Now I ran, ran fast, from fear. It seemed like the whole world was starting to crumble around us. Why? What had we done? What had Joe Steppart ever done bad to anybody?

Before I knew it, I was flying into the house, gasping out the news to my brothers and sisters. "You're not making this up, are you, J.C.?" Sylvester said, shaking his finger at me.

"I swear," I said.

They believed me, then.

"What does it mean, Sylvester?" Laverne said.

Sylvester didn't say anything. Laverne kept on asking him, and the others joined in, but he just shook his head. He was a lot like my daddy, and I was more like my momma. Unless my daddy was sure of what he was saying, he hardly ever talked, except maybe when he was real happy on the way home from church. His life had been hard, but he accepted it. He had told me once that he looked on it as a test. My momma was different. She always had something to say, was always stirring things up just when they'd quiet down, looking for something better for all of us.

Christmas Day, 1919, my daddy accepted that, too. He walked through the door nearly three hours later, my mother behind him, holding onto his hand. "You tell 'em, Emma," he said to her. "It's your idee."

My momma walked into the middle of the room, so she was about the same space from each of us. Her eyes caught mine first, then she looked at each of the others, slow. At the end, her eyes came back to me.

"J.C., go and untie the mule and run him over to Mr. Clannon's. And don't dawdle. Sylvester, you take the rest of the boys, get together all the tools, every one of 'em, and carry them to the Clannons. While you doin' that, me and the girls will be washing down this house."

"Why, Momma?" one of the girls asked.

" 'Cause Emma Owens don't like to leave no dirty house for someone else to live in."

"Someone else!"

"That's right, child," my mother said. "Now when you boys come back, everyone's to get their meager belongin's together and tie 'em up tight."

"We has to be outta here," my father said, "before sundown."

I ran to my mother's side. "But where're we gonna go, Momma?"

She put one wiry hand around my neck and pulled me to her. My momma was a small woman, I wasn't that much shorter than she was even then. And she had the littlest feet I'd ever seen. My father was a big man, and I got my strength from him later on. But even when I grew tall and powerful, my own feet stayed small—as if to say that on the bottom line, I was like my momma, always seeking.

"We're goin' on a train," she answered.

"And where's the train gonna take us, Momma?" I asked right back.

My momma laughed out loud and pulled my ear. "J.C.," she said, "you are the one. Always you got more questions than you got answers, don't you?"

I looked up into her eyes, and nodded. "Where's the train gonna take us, Momma?"

All at once, her face turned serious, almost grim. She let go of me, looked around at the others and then back into my eyes. "It's gonna take us to a better life," she said with her teeth almost clenched.

Later on, I would compete against champions. I would battle toe to toe against a dictator who wanted to rule the entire world, not just a little part of Alabama like Mr. Clannon, but I would never see more "gonna" anywhere than I saw then and there in my momma's two eyes. Everyone else kind of held their breath when she said it. It stopped me, too, for a minute. But then I leaned close to her and, as quietly as I could because I didn't want to make her mad, I asked one more question: "Is the better life in Montgomery, Momma?"

She stared at me hard for a second, and I didn't know which way she'd go, but then that smile that was even bigger than her face showed. "No, J.C." she answered. "It's a lot farther. It's so far that I guess they even have one of those—how do you call them—koll—"

"Kolledge!"

"Kolledge," my mother repeated. "And who knows? The Lord willing—and a little extra do and not so much talk by you—and you just might end up going to one someday. But I'll tell you one thing," she dropped her voice down and brought her head real close to mine, yet so that the others could still hear, "if you don't take that mule over to the boss, that mule gonna die of old age, and if he dies of old age Mr. Clannon ain't gonna pay us three and half dollars for him and if Mr. Clannon doesn't pay us three and a half dollars for him—" Her voice all at once got loud. "Then some folks ain't gonna be able to get on that train, and you sure are gonna be one of those left behind! Now git!"

I raced out of the house. I knew my momma would never leave me behind anywhere. But I'd learned from her that there comes a time when even those who ask the most questions have to stop asking for a while and do what they've got to do. Besides, what other questions were there? I was going to kolledge!

Kolledge.

I was running so fast that I ran right into my father, who must have gone outside while momma was talking. I said my sorry to him and he said not to pay it no mind, just to hurry and get the mule over to the Clannons.

He put his fingers on my shoulder as he said it, but he took them off quick.

Both his hands were shaking, and he couldn't seem to make them stop.

A youth, who bore, 'mid snow and ice,
A banner with a strange device,
Excelsior!

CHAPTER THREE

My father had made good on his prayer. Going north was the hardest thing for him to do.

It wasn't just leaving the only way he knew, and the only way his father and his father's father before him knew, to survive. And it wasn't just leaving the land he loved—loved in spite of how hard it was on him, like you love something you battle with so long that it becomes a part of you. No, it was that, except for us, his family, he was cut off from everything he had known. Where for him, there had been no way to leave, for my mother there was no way to turn back—and so we traveled not merely to the nearest big city, or even to the next state, but all the way north, till land stopped at so much water that no bridge could span it.

Cleveland was a different world.

Was it a better world? It seemed like it, most always.

We did better, as a family. There was work for almost all of us—beloved work! No, it wasn't good pay, and it was menial. But it was honest, steady, and if it paid pennies, at least that was more than just the food on the table we'd gotten from Mr. Clannon. It took awhile, but one day I owned not just a shirt for everyday and a shirt for Sunday, but three shirts. And we didn't have to make all our own furniture. Best of all, though it took two years, the food our labor put on the table was better—meat once a week!

My mother was a maid. My older sisters were, too. Momma set up an incredible schedule so that there would always be someone home to take care of whoever was home, but so that everyone could work as much as possible, too. She only made thirty cents an hour, and my sisters a nickel or a dime less, yet it added up. People were glad to have my momma cleaning their houses because she was honest, and no one scrubbed a floor down like she did. And just to make sure there was no competition, as soon as she found out the going price for maids, she asked for 25 per cent less right off. Little as she was, she never got tired—and momma let my sisters know that they'd better not get tired, either!

My brothers found odd jobs on the same level, from unloading freight cars to part-time janitors. One by one, they had to drop out of school to help bring enough money in for all of us, but at least the money was there. And one by one, because they'd been trained for hard labor by my father in the fields, their part-time jobs started becoming more and more regular. Even I was able to eventually bring home almost a dollar a week, from delivering groceries, working in a greenhouse, all sorts of things.

Only my father, who wanted to work more than any of us, had trouble finding jobs. He couldn't be a maid, and while he was willing to do the most menial tasks like my brothers, he was hardly ever hired. First, he was over forty years old. And also, my brothers had learned a little reading and writing, which you were beginning to need even in unloading boxes off of a freight car. My daddy wouldn't have even been able to read his own name, if somebody had written it down before his eyes. So the only job he got with any consistency, and there were months when he wasn't even able to get that, was that of a garbage man. More days than not, he would spend his time looking for work instead of working. When he did have something, he brought home less than my mother and, soon, less than his own children. But, hard as it was on him, he never said a word, never said what we all thought whenever we'd see him come back from another place where he'd been turned down, with that look on his face: Things had been better for him in Oakville.

There was no doubt though that, all in all, things were better for the Henry Owens family in Cleveland, Ohio. The year even came when we bought our Christmas tree, and decorated it with more than our socks or the wrapping paper that the white people had thrown into their wastebaskets.

My mother tried to make dad feel tolerable about it—the rest of us never dared mention it—saying it was Oakville that got us here, and the right thing would come to him once he got used to the new world up north. But Christmas followed Christmas, without my daddy ever finding regular work.

Yet if I and my brothers and sisters felt pain for him whenever we saw that look on his face, we were too busy to think about it most other times. For me in particular, life was getting more and more exciting. I loved school. But I fell in love with more than school. At the age of nine, believe it or not, I met an unusual little girl named Ruth. She was unusual because even though I knew her family was as poor as ours, nothing she said or did seemed touched by that. Or by prejudice. Or by anything the world said or did. It was as if she had something inside her that somehow made all that not count. I fell in love with her some the first time we ever talked, and a little bit more every time after that until I thought I couldn't love her more than I did. And when I felt that way, I asked her to marry me, even though we were only in the fourth grade, and she said she would.

I didn't think anything could be as exciting as that. But, lo and behold, the year that I entered fifth grade, something happened which—to be honest about it—took over my mind and feelings so completely that whole days would pass when I didn't think of anything else.

My school, which had whites and Negroes together, used the nearby high school coach to teach gym. I'd noticed him watching me for a year or so, especially when we'd play games where there was running or jumping. But he never said anything out of the ordinary until one day, he took me aside.

"Your name's Jesse, am I right?"

I nodded.

"How would you like to be on the track team when you get into high school, Jesse?"

"I would! I would!"

Mr. Riley smiled. You could tell he liked someone with a lot of enthusiasm. I figured that was why he was asking me—though what a surprise it was—because I sure didn't have much talent. Oh, Cleveland had been good for my health and I was starting to grow pretty tall for my age, and running errands and delivering for the grocery store after school had helped my wind, but I was still one of the thinnest kids in the school and surely not one of the fastest.

"Well, then," he said, "you'll have to do more than we do in gym class. Are you willing?"

"Sure." Was I willing!

He told me what I'd have to do, which added up to running and doing some exercises for about an hour and a half every day after school, and I listened with my eyes wide, nodding at everything he said. It was only after he'd finished with, "Well, then, see you tomorrow, Jesse," and walked away, that it suddenly struck me: I worked every day after classes.

I ran faster than I even had that last day in Oakville through the fields looking for my parents, so I could find Mr. Riley. I caught up with him as he was leaving the school. "Mr. Riley, sir," I gasped, "I can't run after school."

"How come?"

"I work. I deliver groceries. Two days I run errands.

Another day I work in the greenhouse over on Simpson Street."

For a second or two, he didn't say anything, kind of weighing what I'd told him. Then the smile came right back onto his face. "That's no problem," he said. "You'll run before school, won't you?"

And that's just what I did. Every morning, just like in Alabama, I got up with the sun, ate my breakfast even before my mother and sisters and brothers, and went to school, winter, spring and fall alike to run and jump and bend my body this way and that for Mr. Charles Riley. And I became stronger, faster, better for it. The progress wasn't something you could measure day by day, but as the weeks and months passed, it was something no one could miss. Little, skinny, sickly J.C. all at once was growing up to be an athlete.

One night at dinner, everyone started talking about it, as I guess had to happen sometime, and Sylvester challenged me to a running race. We went outside just as the sun was about to go down, and walked to the end of the block. The rest of the family was in front of our house at the other end, and when Sylvester and I saw my father raise his hands in the air, we both started.

And I beat him.

"James Cleveland," my father said, putting his arm around me, "you've turned into some kind of boy."

"Jesse's what they call me, Daddy," I said.

I never dreamed what his reaction might be. I was so used to being called Jesse that it had begun to seem strange to be called J.C. or my real given name at home. But he took his hand away and stepped back, like

I'd struck him. "But your name is James Cleveland, J.C. for short," he said.

"But J.C. sounds like Jesse, Daddy," I told him, "and that's what they started calling me at school. Everybody does. Mr. Riley, especially."

My father didn't talk for a minute, and everyone else was strangely silent. Then he put his hand back on my shoulder, but it was in a way he'd never done before. It was as if I wasn't a child any more. "James Cleveland," he said slowly, "if Mr. Riley—and everybody—call you Jesse and you wants to be called Jesse—then that's your name."

It seemed like a happy moment. It was, in one way. I don't think I'd be telling this story today if it hadn't been for Cleveland, and for Charles Riley. But I wouldn't be telling it either, if it weren't for my father, who knelt outside that humble door in Oakville, and prayed for me and with me until my very blood stopped pouring out of my body. And, though I didn't know it then and there, I sensed in the tone of my father's words, that sometimes when you gain something in life, you can lose something, too.

I knew all the things we'd gained from coming to Cleveland. But the things we lost, or were losing, weren't as glaring in the early years there. My father's loss of the land that he, and his father and grandfather before him, had worked. The times on Sunday when, no matter how poor and hungry we'd been the week before, we all walked back the nine miles from church, the eleven of us alone together, talking about our dreams to each other. We didn't go to church every

Sunday now, and we didn't always talk about our dreams. Maybe part of that was because they were coming true.

But part of it was something lost.

That day, though it didn't seem to matter very much, I had lost my name.

Someday, I would discover that I had lost much, much more. And it would matter—more than life itself.

His brow was sad; his eye beneath,
Flashed like a falchion
from its sheath. . . .

CHAPTER FOUR

Sometimes the reason that you lose something and hardly even know you're losing it is because you're moving too fast.

But it was almost impossible for me not to. One step at a time—no, one stride at a time—my life was becoming a race. First against my classmates. Then against other athletes from other schools, all over the United States. And finally, against time itself.

Charles Riley, already past fifty when I came to Cleveland, saw beneath my sickly skin and spindly skeleton, somehow saw my father's long, lion-spring legs and my granddaddy's tireless lungs. But he saw something else, too—what every athlete, and every human being, has inside—the instinct to slack off, give in to the pain and give less than your best, and wish to win through things falling right, or your opponents not doing their best, instead of going to the limit, past your limit, where victory is always found. Because it's victory over yourself.

Someway, Mr. Riley had found the secret of winning that victory anew for himself each day, and for helping others to win it. You couldn't move him when it came to principles, but he hardly ever talked about them—didn't talk much at all, in fact. If you were doing your best, all he did was give you that smile. And if you weren't, he just had some little saying to fit the situation.

There was this first time I ran in competition, for instance. He'd gotten me ready for almost three years, and I wanted so much to win. The race was a quarter of a mile. Mr. Riley often had me run that distance so the eighth of a mile "220" and the 100-yard dash would seem short to me. Though I didn't know that, then. All I knew was that I wanted to win. And for a while, I thought I would! I got off to a fast start, was in front, and when you're in front, it's much easier to do your best. But after about 100 yards, the faint footsteps of the others behind me became louder, louder. I gave an extra burst then, hoping to beat them down, discourage them, and for an instant I thought I had. But that was only because one or two of my opponents had dropped back. The others were still coming, and I knew that nothing would discourage them. When they drew almost even with me, I could see who they were out of the corner of my right eye. Both were two years ahead of me. They were older, stronger, more experienced. I tried not to let it bother me, set my jaw hard, clenched my teeth, narrowed my eyes and gave all I had.

Or I thought I gave all I had.

Once they passed me, though it was only by inches, I knew I'd never be ahead of them again. There was only fifty yards to run. Then twenty. It all goes so fast—and character makes the difference when it's close. At the finish line, I was beaten by both, so I eased up just a bit, and the third runner got there just before I did. I didn't even wind up with the third place ribbon.

It took me almost half an hour to get up the courage to walk over to Mr. Riley and talk about it. He was standing off alone, setting up hurdles for the next race which was coming up. I waited for him to say something, but he didn't. He didn't smile either, though. So finally I said it, "I thought I'd win, Mr. Riley. I should've. Why didn't I?"

Then he smiled, and turned to me. "Because you tried to stare them down instead of run them down, Jesse," he said.

"I don't get it," I said. "What do you mean?"

He smiled again. "I'm not going to tell you, I'm going to show you. Do you work Sunday afternoons, too?"

"No, just in the morning and then I can do what I want the whole day."

"Well, I'll pick you up in front of your house at one o'clock."

"Where are we going?"

"We're going to watch the best runners in the whole world. I'll pick you up at one."

Talk about excited! I counted the minutes until Sunday. That Mr. Riley cared that much about my running—and that I was going to see the best in the whole world. But how could that be? I was getting good enough at reading to go over the sports section of the newspaper that was in the school library, and the best runners in the world weren't anywhere near Cleveland. How could we go see them and get back in time for school Monday?

Mr. Riley picked me up in his old car right on time, and we started driving east. He didn't say anything, just kind of looked at the trees and the clouds and once in a while at me and smiled. Finally, I couldn't stay silent any more and I asked him, "How far is it?"

"Far enough."

I think it was maybe two hours later when he parked the car by a big place with no roof. I didn't know what was going on when he paid for both of us and we went inside. It was horse races!

He took me right down to the fence, so I'd be up close. "I want you to watch these horses run," he said. "No man in the world can come close to them. I want you to watch whichever one in particular takes the lead and holds it. I want you to look at two things. The horse's face. And how the horse's body moves."

I did what he said. Race after race, I watched. And I learned. And when we got back in the car, when the sun had gone down and all the races were over, he asked me to tell him what I'd learned.

"Well, the way they move—the legs and the whole bodies of the horses that can get the lead and keep it—is like they're not trying. Like it's easy. But you know they are trying."

"And what about their faces?"

I thought for a minute. "I don't know," I said. "I didn't see anything on their faces."

He smiled as wide as I'd ever seen. "That's right, Jesse," he said. "Horses are honest. No animal has ever told a lie. No horse has ever tried to stare another one down. That's for actors." He stopped talking, looked hard at me to see if I understood. Then he went on. "And that's what you were doing the other day. Acting. Trying to stare down the other runners. Putting your energy into a determined look on your face. Instead of putting it into your running. Do you know why the best horses make it look easy? Because the determination is all on the inside where no one can see it."

We didn't say another word the whole way home. When he drove up to my house, I thanked him, and he gave me a wide smile and said he'd see me tomorrow. He'd already said all he had to say. And I never forgot it. Every time I ran or jumped, the first thing I remembered was that I wasn't an actor, I was an athlete. The determination, every last bit of it that I could get up, had to be on the inside. But the day came when I did it, put more determination together than I ever had, and was beaten so bad I felt humiliated.

It was my first race against the other high schools in the larger Cleveland area. I was only in my second year, but I was getting good—good enough to be one of two runners Mr. Riley chose to run the 220-yard dash against the best guys from the other schools. For weeks, I'd done nothing but get ready for it physically and mentally. I was going to give everything.

Everything. No—I was going to give more than everything. That was the secret. And then, when I thought I'd given even more than was humanly possible, I was going to reach back somewhere inside myself, like the best race horses did, and find whatever it is on the bottom line that makes a champion, and was going to give it that.

And I'd win.

I suspended every cell of my body on the precipice in that split second before the starter's gun went off. And I got out in front because of it. It was a circular track, with exactly once around being 220 yards, and as soon as I was in the lead, instead of running just fast enough to keep the other runners in back of me, I pushed, but smoothly, like the best race horse I'd seen a year before with Mr. Riley, and widened my lead. And next I did that thing which you only know how to do after you have run hundreds of races, where you gave everything you had every time. I gave it everything I had for about fifty yards, without giving it that burst that you can't have constantly in a 220-yard race. Only in 100-yard dashes or shorter is it possible to go all-out every tenth of a second, and even then it's almost impossible. But I did give everything that I should have given during that part of the race, and I felt my lead growing, widening. When I moved into the second curve before the last, long straightaway, I knew I was supposed to "coast" as fast as I could. Instead, I gave it everything one more time. You were supposed to lay back a little bit at that point so that you'd have something left for the final, grueling straightaway, but I decided that that was when I'd reach back and find something even I didn't know I had. Now, I was giving everything, going as fast as I could, trying to lengthen my lead even more—each fraction of a second feeling like a little eternity as I drove my legs harder, asked for more and more from my lungs and heart.

And then suddenly I was into the straightaway. And when I should have been tiring, I was running faster than I ever had. I should have been leaving them all behind . . . but they were catching up . . . I could hear their spikes digging in louder and louder behind me . . . but this time I didn't give up . . . drove harder . . . reached back farther . . . farther . . . and found that something that you're never sure is there until you take the risk of reaching back all the way—and they drew almost even with me—four of them!

I met their challenge. I raced them head to head, stride for stride, trying harder and harder and harder, trying even harder than that when, almost as a team, they pulled slightly in front of me, then farther, farther.

No! I wouldn't let them beat me. No . . . I have to catch up, I screamed at myself inside . . . have to . . . must. . . .

And I was!

I was on their heels. And, I was almost pulling even with the one who had dropped a half a step behind the other three. I was pulling even . . . passing him . . . pulling even with the next two—

The race was over. The tape at the finish line fluffed across my chest with that familiar, depressing looseness. Even then, some reflex made me keep running just as hard, even though I felt embarrassed because I was doing it, but couldn't stop until I passed them, like there was a chain reaction inside me that trying so hard had set into motion. I didn't stop until I went into the schoolyard wall. I only bruised one elbow.

I didn't feel the pain. The pain of trying my best and being beaten was too great. All I wanted was to get out of there, be alone. I wondered if I had what it took to be able to stand giving everything for the first time in my life and losing.

But before I knew it, Charles Riley was running up to me—and he hardly ever ran himself, liked to take long walks—and was shaking my hand.

"Congratulations, Jesse," he said with great drama. I couldn't speak, just looked up at him, trying to understand. I knew he'd never make fun of me.

"I know, I know," he answered what my eyes had asked. "You think you lost today. But you're as wrong about that as you were about those determined looks you used to put on your face. You won today. And you know who you beat? You didn't beat him once, either, you beat him a hundred times out there. Even when the race was over, you didn't stop. You beat him one more time." Coach Riley was talking more than I'd ever heard him. "And I'm going to tell you something else, something I've never said to anyone. Tomorrow's a new day, and because you beat your opponent today doesn't mean that you'll beat him tomorrow. And next week is a new week. Same thing. And next year. But—" His voice dropped almost to a whisper. "If you do beat him again tomorrow, and again next week, and again next year, and you keep on winning over him, you'll go to the Olympics someday! But even if you were as fast as those race horses we saw, it won't get you there unless you can win like you won today. You know who you beat, don't you?"

I knew. It didn't need to be said. And I knew I was going to the Olympics someday, impossible as it seemed a few minutes before.

Yet what I didn't know was that the same person I would triumph over time and time again to get there—Jesse Owens—would, soon after the Olympics, pass me at the finish line. Because I would unknowingly give in to that deep, half-hidden wish within that the Olympics are the Olympics.

They aren't.

Life—the inner life—is the true Olympics. So, as I unceasingly worked—no, slaved—to become faster and faster, jump farther and farther, as the taut tape at the finish line began becoming familiar to me, and then something that happened every time, as my name got in the papers and even started to get in some record books, each stride which took me closer to the Olympic Games was simultaneouly taking me farther and farther away from what was good about Oakville. The more I achieved, the more my father's pain became painful to me—so painful that I began turning away from it instead of reaching out to him. Sunday morning began to mean less and less, too. Oh, I believed in God, but did I need Him as much? I mean, if I could do all this myself—

I think Charles Riley saw what was happening before anyone else. He was a very spiritual man, who never intruded on you with his belief, but who didn't let any of his boys intrude on God either. Once our star shot putter thought he'd broken the school record and won first place to boot, when the referee called a foul on him for going out of the circle. The athlete got mad and said, "Goddamn you!" to the ref. He was going to say more, too, but suddenly Charles Riley appeared out of nowhere, stood between the two of them, and glared into this boy's eyes with a look I'd never seen before. The boy didn't say another word, but the coach did.

"I don't ever want to hear you talk that way again," Riley told him.

"I'm sorry, Coach," Bill said, still angry, "but I didn't step out of the circle."

"Maybe you did, and maybe you didn't," Charles Riley said. "But you just stepped out of a much bigger circle. If I ever hear you do it one more time, you're off this track team." Then he turned, and walked away.

I never took the name of the Lord in vain, partly because my father and mother had brought us up that way. But, happy as the coach was with all my victories and records, I knew there was something bothering him about me. The feeling grew even stronger when I wasn't with him than when I was. Over the summer between my third and my last year of high school, it was as if he was there—though I didn't see him once—trying to tell me something. But with all the jobs I held, the running and jumping I was doing on my own to keep in shape, my family—and Ruth—I could never quite make out the "message" I sensed he was trying to send me.

I decided that when I got back to school, I would just ask him outright. Yet when I saw him that first day in September of 1931, I couldn't. Charles Riley was the kind of man who would say something to you when he wanted to, and only then. So the whole year passed, the year of an unbroken string of victories, many of which broke some other athlete's long-held string of records, without ever once talking man-to-man. A few days before the final competition of the season, I told him of all the scholarship offers I'd had from colleges—*kolledges!*—all over the country. "I'd like your advice if you'd be willing to give it to me," I said.

"Why don't you come to my office the last day of school," he answered.

When I walked into his office that day, he was reading the Bible. I've never known whether it was an accident or deliberate. But as he looked up to greet me and to put the book down, a piece of paper fell out and sailed this way and that, going lower and lower each time, until strangely, it landed exactly at my feet.

I bent down to pick it up, glanced at it before offering it back to him. It was a poem by Longfellow, called *Excelsior*.

And instead of taking it from me, he held up his hand and said, "No, Jesse, it landed at your feet. Keep it. I know it by heart, anyway. Read it someday, when you feel the need."

I folded up the piece of paper and put it in my wallet. And then we talked about the dozens and dozens of scholarship offers I had received, even though I was a Negro. Some offered tuition, some offered that plus room and board, some even hinted at cars and extra money and much more. And most all I'd have to take would be some Phys Ed courses. "Which one should I go to?" I asked.

"None of them," he said flatly. "I think you should pay your own way."

And like a silver clarion rung
The accents of that unknown tongue,
Excelsior!

CHAPTER FIVE

In the early 1830s, my ancestors were brought on a boat across the Atlantic Ocean from Africa to America as slaves for men who felt they had the right to own other men.

In August of 1936, I boarded a boat to go back across the Atlantic Ocean to do battle with Adolf Hitler, a man who thought all other men should be slaves to him and his Aryan armies.

The journey to Berlin had begun almost twenty-three years before in Oakville, carrying me to Cleveland, and then to Columbus and Ohio State University, where I took Charles Riley's advice and paid my own way, holding three jobs, just like before. In that time, the Henry Owens family had journeyed, too. Through time. There were no more children now. All of us had grown up. Prentice, my oldest brother, was almost as old as my father had been when I was a little boy in Oakville, married, with children who were starting to grow up. Almost all my other brothers and sisters were married, too, and had children. And so did I.

As a matter of fact, I had married before many of them. The little girl I had met, the pigtailed girl without prejudice, had become my wife secretly when we were only sixteen years old.

We had to do it secretly, of course, because neither my momma and daddy or hers would ever have let us. You couldn't get married that young in Ohio without your parents' consent, so one of my high school buddies, Dave Albritton, somehow got hold of a car for one day on a rainy Saturday in April, and we drove into Pennsylvania, stopping at every town until we found a Justice of the Peace who would make us man and wife. Dave was our witness and best man and, with what the license cost and money for the gas we had to put in the borrowed car, all we had left over for a wedding dinner was enough money for one hot dog sandwich between the three of us. We each loaded our part of it with a ridiculous amount of relish on every small bite, and by the time we got back to Cleveland, we all had stomach aches. There was no honeymoon. We weren't even going to be able to live together. Dave and I dropped Ruth off late as it was, then brought the car back to his buddy, and I ran the ten miles home as fast as my legs would carry me. When I walked in, I had a lot of explaining to do—and it couldn't be explained. So I simply took my mother's wrath as it exploded for almost an hour. Punctuality and cleanliness, she'd always felt, were strongly connected to the more important virtues. The years may have lined her face and grayed her hair some, but her shout when she was angry still seemed as loud as Gabriel's horn.

The years seemed to have taken more toll on my daddy. His hair had gone almost completely white, and you noticed it because his skin was much darker than my momma's or mine, and he didn't seem nearly as tall as he once was. It wasn't just age, because his spirit seemed bent over, too. He hadn't changed any of his values or ways. So his spirit was the same—just bent over a little, maybe because it had to or else it would have broken. When I entered college, I asked only one thing in return for giving up all the scholarships: If a job ever opened up on campus, that they'd give my father first crack at it. It took almost a year, but finally a position was vacant—combination groundskeeper--maintenance man. It was Henry Owens' first regular job since sharecropping in Oakville. I hoped it would make him happy, somehow make up for those fifteen long years of a few hours or a few days doing odd jobs or temporary garbage collecting wherever he could find it. But, though he gladly accepted and threw himself into it, I honestly think it came too late.

For me, on the other hand, things seemed to be happening too early and so fast that I could hardly keep up with them. As the time neared to board the ship that would take me across the Atlantic Ocean so that I could go to Berlin in the 1936 Olympics, I was shocked one morning when I realized that I was sitting at the breakfast table with Ruth and the baby, with the newspaper there on the table with my picture right on the front page. What shocked me wasn't that my picture was on the front page.

It was that I'd gotten used to seeing it there.

"I'd like for us to go to church before I leave on that boat, Baby," I said to her.

"I'm glad to hear you say that, Jesse," she answered. "It's been a long time since you said that."

I thought out loud. "Can't this morning—got to meet Coach Snyder at ten—maybe next Sunday morning, but I've got that press conference and got to get in my practice sometime. We wouldn't have to go in the morning—could go at night."

But one busy morning became another, days fled like minutes till, before I knew it, I was kissing Ruth goodbye and getting ready to leave with the American Olympic Team for New York. "I'll pray for you, Jesse," she said.

Ruth was different than my mother in one way—she never pushed. But somehow, she always said whatever was needed to let you know exactly what she thought. "We never did make it to church, did we?" I said a little sadly, and maybe a little scared. "Next time, Baby."

I didn't think about it again, frankly, till the ship left New York. Then, as the last traces of land vanished, and I knew we were moving farther and farther from America and that I wouldn't see it again until I had won or I had lost, as I looked in every direction and could only see an infinity of ocean stretching before my eyes, I had the almost overwhelming impulse to drop down on my knees and thank God for letting me come to this opportunity, and to ask His help to make the most of it.

But I didn't.

Was it because my teammates were around? Or a bunch of strangers? Or was it because there was a stranger inside of me now?

I was brought up with a belief in God and the teachings of Jesus—His Word—to have His Spirit—to believe, to know, that if we struggled to the utmost and climbed the highest mountains within ourselves, that above the final summit He would be there.

Why would God desert me now? No, He wouldn't leave me now. I had married and fathered a child. I had run as fast and jumped as far as any man in the world. I had gone to a fine university and learned to read some of the most learned books in it. But I had not learned the great truth that God never leaves us.

We leave Him.

In happy homes he saw the light
Of household fires gleam
warm and bright . . . .

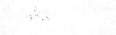

CHAPTER SIX

If I wasn't up to getting down on my knees and praying on the ship, showing in public what I believed seemed to be even more out of the question once I'd left the ship and arrived in Berlin.

It was a godless city. Oh, there must have been some who believed, who secretly didn't go along with Hitler's ideas that he and his atheistic master race were superior to the rest of the world—but I and no one else would ever know it because they'd have to keep it secret. For some, though, it was impossible to keep their beliefs hidden. The Jewish people, for example, were known to have their own firm and devout religion. Before another Olympiad would ever take place, millions of them would be put to death by the German dictator for that religion.

But during the 1936 Olympics, Hitler had an even

better target than the Jews—the United States Olympic team. First, a big part of Hitler's superiority idea was that his Nazis should rule not just because they were better and smarter, but because they were stronger and healthier. Though Hitler himself was short, dark, and anything but athletic-looking, he constantly talked of his "tall, blond, blue-eyed, Aryan supermen." Every newspaper was filled with his braggings of how the German Olympic team would prove him correct by "vanquishing the inferior Americans."

But when Hitler said "inferior Americans," he meant more than that. Our track and field squad—and the running and jumping events seemed to get more publicity than all the other sports put together—in 1936 happened to be made up mostly of Negro stars. My buddy, Dave Albritton, was there. So was Ralph Metcalfe and others. And all of us came from pretty much the same background—Southern poor, physical laboring, God fearing. We were everything Hitler hated. Other people—the Jews, Poles, and all the others Hitler hungered to have abjectly kneeling at his feet—at least didn't have their beliefs written on their very skins.

But, in particular, Hitler hated my skin. For I happened to have been the one who had set world records in the 100- and 200-yard dashes less than a year before, and had been dubbed "the world's fastest human" because of it. Even more, I happened to have broken the world broad-jump record by more than half a foot. Much before I was ever in the headlines, Hitler's critics outside of Germany—none were left inside—had challenged him to point to one person who was the super-strong, super-smart, super-everything Aryan superman. Hitler would have his henchmen answer that he was raising a race of his Aryan armies. But now, newspapermen from all over the world were asking him, "Who have you got to beat Jesse Owens?"

I wanted no part of politics. And I wasn't in Berlin to compete against any one athlete. The purpose of the Olympics, anyway, was to do your best. As I'd learned long ago from Charles Riley, the only victory that counts is the one over yourself.

But Adolf Hitler wouldn't allow me that. He made the victory over myself and victory over another man one and the same when, finally, after years of being asked who was the supreme example of his Aryan superman, Hitler answered with a name.

Luz Long was that name.

It came as a shock to me that Hitler would name anybody. I'd heard of Long, of course. The Germans didn't let the rest of the world know exactly what their athletes were doing, so I had no idea how good he was. But there was no doubt that he was good. Our team had also heard that Hitler was keeping some super-athlete under wraps completely for the games. Obviously, Long was the one. I wondered what he looked like. And could he be the superman that Hitler claimed? One thing I did know: Luz Long had been groomed his entire life for this Olympiad, and for only a single event in it. The broad jump.

It was about fifteen minutes after I first set foot in

Berlin's huge stadium on a muggy, August day, when I felt a strange, ominous chill run through me as my eyes scanned the athletes from other countries and then stopped cold on one who was wearing the German uniform. I knew it was Luz Long. And he indeed was a supreme example of Aryan perfection. Taller than I was by an inch, maybe two, the blue-eyed, sandy-haired Long was one of those rare athletic happenings you come to recognize after years in competition—a perfectly proportioned body, every lithe but powerful cord a celebration of pulsing natural muscle, stunningly compressed and honed by tens of thousands of obvious hours of sweat and determination. He may have been my archenemy, but I had to stand there in awe and just stare at Luz Long for several seconds.

Yet when he walked over to the broad-jump area to take a practice leap I knew—though it was the last thing I wanted to admit to myself—that he had the competitive spirit to match his body. Long didn't jump. He exploded with such an intensity, yet such ease. I was suddenly reminded of the race horses Charles Riley had taken me to see.

Long landed, laughing. One of the jumpers from another country came up to me. "You're lucky this is practice," he said matter-of-factly. "If they were measuring what that German did, it might be a new record."

And it might have been.

And, soon, too soon, they were measuring.

And for the first time in years I was falling short.

The broad-jump trials gave each athlete three tries to

make a qualifying distance of 24 feet, 6 inches. I hadn't gone less than a foot further than that, practice or otherwise, for two years. And my first jump went much more than a foot further.

But I fouled.

In my eagerness to show Luz Long what I had, I'd been careless about measuring my steps to the take-off board. I'd gone over it.

Forget it, I said to myself. *You've fouled before. There are still two jumps left.*

I told myself that, but I didn't believe it. Second by second, home seemed farther away. Much more than the 6,000 miles. I wanted to be here, in Berlin, in the Olympics, but it wasn't my turf. It was Luz Long's turf. He was safe here. I was safe in Cleveland. Even in Oakville. Was poverty so bad after all? You didn't starve and at least it was familiar. That kind of empty stomach was a lot better than this kind—the kind I felt now—strange empty—the kind you knew wouldn't be filled at six o'clock dinner—the kind nothing would fill—

Stop thinking those thoughts! I screamed silently to myself. It took a few more unheard shouts, but I finally got myself together. I overcame the impulse to really fly. Instead, I measured my steps with absolute precision. Once. Then again. And as I jumped, when my name was finally called after all the waiting, I didn't try to break any records or outdo Luz Long. I tried just to qualify. That's all I wanted—just to get into the finals, and have three jumps again.

And I fell short by three inches. I was almost in a state

of shock.

I had jumped less than twenty-five feet. I hadn't done that since—since—high school.

I put on my sweatshirt and tried to get off by myself. The reporters were buzzing around me like locusts. The press had always been good to me, and I tried to be as good as I could in return, but all my nerves now were like open wounds with each question cutting deeper and deeper. Finally, I'd answered their questions the best I could and they'd all gone to file their stories. All except one. He was an American writer I'd gotten to know pretty well.

"Jesse, off the record," he said when we were alone, "is it true about Hitler?"

"Is what true?"

"That he walked out of the stadium on you. Look—" The reporter pointed to Hitler's plush box in the first row center. It was glaringly empty. For a second I didn't know what to say. "I don't know," was all I could answer.

"That's what I heard, anyway," he said. "Anyhow, I'm going to file the story—won't quote you, though. It was right before your first practice jump. Saw it myself. Then I asked a couple of the German athletes, and they said that Hitler had made some vow not to look at you in action. Crazy?"

I nodded. But without much conviction. Was he crazy? I had just one jump left. And almost no time to get ready for it. The broad-jump preliminaries came before the finals of the other three events I was in—the 100-meter and 200-meter dashes, and the relay. How I did in the next ten minutes—with this one remaining chance—was, I knew, how I would do in the entire Olympics.

And, somehow, I sensed, in life itself.

What if I—I stopped myself from thinking it time and again, but it kept crashing through my mind—what if—what if—what if I didn't qualify? Hitler won't look so crazy, then . . . .

I fought, fought hard, harder . . . but, one cell at a time, panic crept into my body, taking me over. Any minute now—maybe any second—my name would be called for the final jump. I looked at Hitler's box. Empty. His way of saying that Jesse Owens was inferior. Around that box, filling every seat, were a hundred thousand Germans. All wanting Luz Long to beat me. And there laughing in a carefree way near the broad-jump pit, was Luz Long. He had only had to take one preliminary jump. Because he'd broken the Olympic record with it. Was he a superman? Even that idea began invading me.

I shook my body like an animal does to shake off water and walked back to the broad-jump area and, as I did, I heard a name called. Mine. Had to get ready because, after the man about to jump had jumped, it would be my turn. I glanced over at him. He was from England or France, I think, the champion of his own country, but he hadn't qualified in his first two jumps, either. And he probably wouldn't make it on this one.

I closed my eyes—didn't want to see him. Because I wasn't really seeing him, I was seeing myself. I heard the familiar sounds of his feet moving quickly toward the runway, the hush as he went up in the air, the disappointed murmurs when he came down far short.

Now it was my turn.

I opened my eyes, closed them once again. *I have to find strength somewhere,* I said to myself. *Have to reach into myself and find the strength to make it, to do my best.*

But there was nothing inside. I could find nothing. I was back in Oakville, except that this time I wasn't starting out in life, no matter how low, I was back there, ending up. I'd reached for the top, and fallen all the way to the bottom. Lower than I'd ever been, so low I'd never be able to get up again.

No.

No.

I can't let it happen. I can't—

But how? *What?* If I jumped with all my might, I'd foul. If I played it safe, I wouldn't go far enough. I've already lost. There's no way—

I must find a way.

Must.

Almost instinctively, I dropped down to my knees. *Pray. Must pray,* I whispered to myself.

But in front of a hundred thousand people?

"Jesse Owens!" It was the loudspeaker announcing my name for the second time.

I closed my eyes, one of my knees touching the ground. *I must pray.*

But what will they all think of me? *I must pray.*

Can't—

Must—

66

Can't—

But I must. Oh, God, I pleaded wordlessly with everything that was inside me. *Help me to pray. God, help me—*

But I couldn't. Couldn't.

"Jesse Owens!" They were calling my name for the last time. I had to get up, jump. But I hadn't prayed.

"Jazze Owenz!" Suddenly I felt a hand on my shoulder. It wasn't the loudspeaker calling my name a final time. It was a man standing right there next to me.

It was Luz Long.

Above, the spectral glaciers shone,
And from his lips escaped a groan,
Excelsior!

CHAPTER SEVEN

My archenemy. Or was he? The way his hand rested on my shoulder, the vibrations I felt as he looked at me and smiled, made me know somehow that, far from being my enemy, he was my friend.

Luz turned out to be the best friend I ever had. He turned out to be what you might call a messenger from God.

Any doubts I had left about him vanished the instant he spoke. "What has taken your goat, Jazze Owenz?" he asked.

In spite of all my panic, I had to smile. Almost laugh. But I couldn't speak.

"I Luz Long," he said, introducing himself. I nodded. "I think I know what is wrong with you," he went on, answering his own question. "You are 100 per cent when you jump. I the same. You cannot do

71

halfway, but you are afraid you will foul again."

"That's right," I said, finding my voice for the first time.

"I have answer," he said. "Same thing happen to me last year in Cologne."

There were literally only seconds left before I had to jump or default. Luz told me to simply remeasure my steps and jump from six inches in back of the take-off board giving it all I had. That way I could give 100 per cent and still not be afraid of fouling. He even laid his towel down at exactly the place from which I was to jump. It was so simple!

And it worked.

I could feel the confident energy surging back into my body as I stood still for that brief second before beginning my run. I went as fast as I ever had, took off, and felt almost like I was flying. When I came down, it was more than 26 feet—an Olympic record—from the take-off board. With the extra six inches, it surely would have been a new unofficial record.

But what did I care about records? I was in the finals!

I didn't know how to thank Luz Long. Because of him, because of his seeing past skin color, nationality, and Hitler's godless beliefs, I had what was most important to me in the world: A chance to rise from Oakville to champion of the entire world.

All I could offer in return was my friendship. I met with him that night, and we talked over coffee in the Olympic Village. We might've stayed up a little later than athletes should, who have to compete against the best from every country in the following days, but it was worth it for the bond between us gave a spiritual strength which was greater than the physical. Luz and I, it turned out, were very much alike. He was married and had one child, too. A son, Karl. He had come from humble beginnings. And he didn't believe Hitler's Aryan supremacy statements and was disturbed by the military aggressiveness of the German dictator. Still, it was his country and he felt that if he didn't fight for it, he would be putting his wife and child in danger.

I asked him about religion. He said that he did not have any, had never really known any. "Do you believe in God?" I questioned.

He held out his hands, palms up, as if to say he didn't know. Then he shrugged a little, as if to add that he had never really had any evidence that there was a higher power. He was so good, and all the truly good people I'd known till then believed in God. But even if Luz was a Nazi who might soon be my archenemy again, trying to kill my countrymen and even me, I felt that beneath that he was my brother. And even though he didn't believe in God, I believed in Luz Long. And nothing would ever change that.

We spent each night afterward talking, and the days competing. Because of him, I won the 100-meter dash and the 200-meter, breaking records in both, and helped to lead my team to victory—and a record—in the relay. But most of all, I was waiting for the high point: The broad jump. For here, once again, Luz and I would be competing against one another. Without him, I would have never been competing at all. Yet I somehow had to fuse that feeling with the will to do my best. For wasn't my love for Luz—and yes, I loved him—a love for the best that is within man, the best that was within me?

The day of the broad jump arrived. One by one, the other finalists fell by the wayside. Then, it was only Luz Long and Jesse Owens.

His first leap took the lead.

I beat it.

His second of three was even better.

I beat it by half an inch.

I watched him take a deep breath before his final leap. I watched his blue eyes look up into the sky, then down, fixing on a point which he knew—and I knew—would be well over an Olympic record. I could see him transforming the same beautiful energy which had enabled him to come to me and change the course of my life when I needed it most into the determination to do what had never been done before—to do what most men would call a miracle.

He stood perfectly still, as still as a statue, for an instant, and only his eyes moved as they looked skyward once more, and then he began his run. Fast from the beginning, not gradual like most, but then faster. His perfectly proportioned legs working like pistons now, his finely honed physique working like one total machine, all for one purpose, for one split second—

And then it happened. High. Higher than I'd ever seen anyone leap. But with so much power that it was not merely high, it was far. Incredibly far.

It seemed for a split second that he would never

come down. But then he did, straining his body more than I'd ever seen any man strain, as if he were an eagle attempting at the last minute to rise above an infinite mountain . . . straining . . . moving forward as he fell downward . . . forward farther . . . forward. . . .

He landed!

Exactly in the spot on which his eyes had fixed.

Luz Long had set a new Olympic record.

I rushed over to him. Hugged him. I was glad. So glad.

But now it was my turn.

I took my time, measured my steps once, then again. I was tense, but that good kind of tense that you feel when you have to be tense to do your best. Deep, deep inside, under all the layers, there was a clear, placid pool of peace.

Now I, too, stood perfectly still.

I, too, looked up at the sky.

Then, I looked into Luz's blue eyes, as he stood off to the side, his face wordlessly urging me to do my best, to do better than I'd ever done. Looking into his eyes was no different than looking into the blue, cloudless sky.

I didn't look at the end of the pit. I decided I wasn't going to come down. I was going to fly. I was going to stay up in the air forever.

I began my run, also fast from the beginning, not gradual like most, but then faster.

I went faster, precariously fast, using all my speed to its advantage. And then!

I hit the take-off board. Leaped up, up, up—

. . . My body was weightless . . . I surged with all I

had but at the same time merely let it float . . . higher . . . higher . . . into the clouds . . . I was reaching for the clouds . . . the clouds . . . the heavens—

I was coming down! Back to earth.

I fought against it.

I kicked my legs.

I churned my arms.

I reached to the sky as I leaped for the farthest part of the ground.

The farthest—

I was on the earth once again. I felt the dirt and the sand of the pit in my shoes and on my legs. Instinctively, I fell forward, my elbows digging in, the tremendous velocity of my jump forcing sand into my mouth.

It tasted good. Because, almost instinctively, I sensed it was the sand from a part of the pit which no one had ever reached before.

Luz was the first to reach me. "You did it! I know you did it," he whispered.

They measured.

I had done it.

I had gone farther than Luz. I had set a new Olympic record. I had jumped farther than any man on earth.

Luz didn't let go of my arm. He lifted it up—as he had lifted me up in a different way a few days before—and led me away from the pit and toward the crowd. "Jazze Owenz!" he shouted. "Jazze Owenz!"

Some people in the crowd responded, "Jazze Owenz!"

Luz shouted it louder. "Jazze Owenz!"

Now a majority of the crowd picked it up. "Jazze
Owenz! Jazze Owenz! Jazze Owenz!" they yelled.

Luz yelled it again. The crowd yelled it again. Luz
again. And now the whole crowd, more than a hundred
thousand Germans, were yelling, "Jazze Owenz! Jazze
Owenz! Jazze Owenz!"

They were cheering me. But only I knew who they
were really cheering.

I lifted Luz Long's arm.

"Luz Long!" I yelled at the top of my lungs. "Luz
Long! Luz Long! Luz Long! Luz Long!"

Yet it wasn't Luz who had lifted me into the heavens
today.

I knew who had brought me from the precipice of
hell to be able to ascend into the heavens today.

It wasn't Jesse Owens. It wasn't anyone who ever
ran, or jumped, or balanced on the precipice of hell.

Luz Long may not have believed in God.

But God had believed in Luz Long.

He had made Luz His sacred messenger.

"Try not the pass,"
the old man said . . . .

CHAPTER EIGHT

Except for having to leave Luz, it seemed that everything in life was perfect now.

And Luz and I had vowed to write and, no matter where life led us, to see each other again someday.

Though I didn't like leaving Luz, I did want to leave Europe, because I missed Ruth, my little daughter Gloria, my parents, brothers and sisters, and home even more. But I didn't get home right away. For now, it seemed, the whole world was my home.

It dawned on me with blinding brightness. After less than a week I realized: I had jumped into another rare kind of stratosphere—one that only a handful of people in every generation are lucky enough to know.

For a time, at least, *I was the most famous person in the entire world.*

Talk about perfection! This was more. Perfection is

everything you ever dreamed of having. This was more.

The sickly little boy from Oakville had never dreamed, for instance, of returning to New York after breaking records in the 1936 Olympics to be welcomed by the mayor, who had a convertible car ready for him to ride through the streets of that city—streets lined with more people than I'd even seen in the German stadium, people wanting only to reach out and touch me, or see me if they couldn't do that, like I was more than a human being. One of them—I never even saw his or her face—actually thrust a plain brown paper bag in my lap as the car cruised between the walls of cheering people. I put it on the floor and didn't look at it until later. It was filled with money! Thousands of dollars. In tens and fives and ones and sometimes twenties. It must have been someone's life savings!

The parade was only the beginning. And the almost five thousand dollars in a brown paper bag seemed like only the beginning of much, much more. There wasn't an hour that some celebrity or millionaire didn't have me at his house or on his boat or at some plush restaurant with all kinds of other important people at the party. I sent for Ruth that night now that I was rich—though I took $2,500 right before that and wired it to a real estate agent in Cleveland as a down payment for a house for my parents. It was something they'd wanted—and they'd never dreamed was possible—all their lives.

Ruth got a kick out of being wined and dined, too, for a couple of days anyway. But then I could tell she was starting to get edgy. She didn't say anything, but Ruth never had to put what she felt into words. So one night I asked her what was on her mind.

"You worked—possibly slaved is the word—Jesse," she said, "for many years for this. And you deserve everything they're saying about you and doing for you. And I sure have eaten more different kinds of food in the last three days than I ever had in my whole life put together. But maybe I should go home before you," she went on.

"These people really aren't our kind."

"You mean Negroes?" I asked.

She shook her head. "You know I don't see it that way, Darling," she answered softly. "Possibly I mean that they won't be around after the party's over."

"But the party's never going to be over," I laughed. "And some of them will be around. Because I'll be working with them. You wouldn't believe some of the jobs that these millionaires have offered me."

She didn't say anything.

"Well, don't you believe me?"

"Of course, I believe you, Jesse."

I tried to persuade her to stay, but the next day she went back. I had to stay—had to decide which millionaire or two I wanted to work with. I told one of them about the money in the brown paper bag, and he'd only slapped me on the shoulder and said, "Owens, you'll have to find a bag as big as the Grand Canyon for what you'll be making soon!"

By the end of that week, though, the money in the paper bag was almost gone. Sure, everyone was picking up the tab for me, but I also found it easy to buy clothes for the family back home, jewelry, and sometimes I even insisted on paying when I ate with the wealthy.

I started trying to press some of the rich men who'd talked big money to me, told them I'd like to sit down at their office instead of in a restaurant or country club. But they just wanted to party with me. "There'll be time for that, there'll be time for that," one of them repeated when I asked him exactly what he had in mind. The sharecropper's kid from Oakville may have gotten an education and become an Olympic athlete, but did I know the ways of big business? Maybe that was the way things were done. But I also knew something else for sure: I had $40.16 left now.

"Look," I told one of them on the phone when I called him at his office the next morning, "I'm going to have to go back to Cleveland tomorrow. You said you wanted me right at the top of your firm. How are we going to talk about it if I'm back in Cleveland?"

He was smooth as silk. I was going to find a lot of them like that. They were like fine, hand-painted ties, being pulled tighter and tighter around your neck. "I do want you right at the top with us, Jesse," he said, talking to me in a tone like he was my own father. "And that's why I don't want you to take anything less. Right at the moment, we only have lesser positions. But as soon as something breaks, I'll call you. What's your phone number in Cleveland?"

I didn't have a phone.

One by one, each of them gave me the same line, only with different words. Every one of them, when they put me off, made it sound like they were doing me a favor. One man, who I heard was worth a hundred million dollars and owned a whole building and had bought out an entire restaurant for one night to have a party for me, was "out of town" every time I called. It was beginning to get to me. There was still a half-hour before five, and I left the hotel and actually sprinted over to his office. He was on the top floor. I was heading down the hall to the main entrance when a door opened right next to me, the door to his private office. He was leaving for home. Or another party for someone else. I was learning fast that even the most famous man in the world doesn't stay the most famous very long.

We actually bumped into one another. "Why, Jesse!" he greeted.

"Mr. Kri—"

"Call me Brad, Jesse," he corrected.

I called him Brad. I asked him about the job he'd talked about. He'd said I'd "fit in" and could be a "real asset" and a lot of other talk.

He looked at me like a man trying to remember something. He wrinkled up his forehead. "Well, sure, you'd be an asset," he said slowly, like he was still trying to remember and couldn't. "No doubt about it. But we didn't say anything definite, did we? You see, I'm not hiring right now."

I was losing my cool. "But you said—"

"Jesse, Jesse, take it easy," he interrupted in a calm tone of voice. "A man with four Olympic gold medals has the world at his feet. And we aren't having one of our best years. Maybe I'll be asking you for a job soon!" He squeezed my arm in a certain way. It was as if to say that we both understood what he was talking about. And I was beginning to understand.

"Say," he added, as we got out of the elevator, "if you're still in town next Thursday, I'm having a bunch of the boys out to my lodge for some—"

"Thanks," I said, "but I'm leaving tomorrow. Thanks."

I didn't run back to my hotel room. But when I got there, I packed quickly. I didn't have enough money for another night. I'd take the bus back instead of the train.

I made sure to cram everything into my suitcase. I had a feeling I couldn't afford to even forget a pair of socks. I came across a copy of the Bible that they have in every hotel room. It had been there all the time, just inches from my head when I went to sleep each night, but I hadn't looked at it once. I looked at it now, stopping at one place to read, and then another.

Eventually, I put it down. I had to leave the room or pay for another night. I'd already stayed past checkout time, but they were making an exception for me. After all, I was still on Page 1 of every newspaper, on the covers of most magazines. And what had it all gotten me? A few extra hours in a lonely hotel room.

I left the hotel to begin walking toward the bus station. I couldn't take a step, not a step, without somebody asking for my autograph or waving to me or saying, "That's Jesse Owens." One of the passages from the Bible that I'd read in the room kept coming back to me as I made my way toward the bus station.

It was from Ecclesiastes.

"Vanity of vanities," it began, "all is vanity."

I got a little sleep in the bus station and when I woke up, I decided to look more positively at things. Ruth was right. Those millionaires had only been there for the party. But everyone couldn't be like them. After all, though I'd won the top prizes in amateur sports, there had to be some way I could use my athletic talents to make a living. And also, I was one year away from a college degree. It wasn't as if I were uneducated. "And I'll work hard, as hard as anyone you've ever seen," I suddenly said aloud. I had only meant to say it in my mind, but it had come out.

The words stayed with me. I knew why. They were the exact same words my father had used trying to get a job in Cleveland for fifteen years.

It's different for me, I said to myself. *When I get back to Cleveland, there'll be something. There'll be something, and I'll find it.*

But when I got back to Cleveland, there was almost nothing. One job and one job alone was offered to me— local playground instructor for twenty-eight dollars a week. Desperate, I took it. At least it put food on the table. I'd finish college later. Right now I had to have anything that would help me and my family to survive, while I looked for something better.

And that something better had better come soon, I knew. I had gone ahead and bought my parents the house. I'd been sure there had to be some good job somewhere for me. How could I take the money back, anyway? There'd been enough for a down payment and the first few monthly payments. The last of that money would be gone in weeks. It would be worse to give my parents a home and then make them move from it, than for them to have had no house at all.

I kept trying, but Cleveland was only so big. There was no place left to go. I'll do anything, I began saying to people. And to myself. Most of them looked away, like they were ashamed I said it. But I meant it. What other choice did I have? As long as it was honest.

My momma used to have a bunch of things she said. One or the other of them would cover just about any situation. "If you look hard enough for the devil, the devil'll find you," was a favorite of hers.

On a Saturday evening, two businessmen came to my house. They reminded me a lot of the millionaires I'd met in New York, except that you could tell they weren't millionaires—only wanted to be. They were promoting Negro baseball (colored people weren't allowed in baseball or football or any of the other professional sports, so I couldn't make a living there) and wanted me to help promote the tour they were launching. When I first heard that, I was more excited than I'd been in months. Here it was—right at the last minute when I needed it most—another opportunity of a lifetime! I hadn't played much baseball, I'd been too busy with track. But I was fast, and strong, and I'd learn. I'd learn.

They stopped me when I began talking like that. "We don't want you to play," one of them said. "We want you to help us promote it. We want you to do something before the game each night."

"What?"

"We want you to race against a horse for 100 yards,"

the other man said. Ruth walked from the room.

"Get out," I told them.

One of them handed me his card. "No hard feelings," he said. "Here's where I can be reached if you change your mind."

"I won't change my mind," I said, looking over at my Olympic gold medals.

I hardly talked to Ruth that weekend, I was so down. I had to figure out something, had to make more money. There were only days left until the next payment on my parents' house was due.

I went to work at the playground Monday, but my heart wasn't in it. No matter how bad I ever felt in my life, being with kids, playing with them and showing them things, sometimes letting them show me, always made me feel good. But that day, it was like I was at the bottom.

I usually ran home to keep myself in shape, but that dusk I could hardly walk. When I reached the entrance to the apartment, there was someone else walking toward me. A tall man, dressed a little different than anything I'd seen. He had a young boy with him. When he spoke, it was with an accent that did but didn't sound British. "Are you Jesse Owens?" he asked with an open, kind face.

"Yes."

He and his boy introduced themselves. They were from Australia—had come all the way from Australia—to meet me.

I had to ask them in. Ruth fixed a little extra for dinner, though we didn't have much, and all of us had a good hour and a half together. It was like an hour in a fantasyland, and I almost forgot my troubles now and then because of the warmth of the man and his son toward me and my family.

But when they left, I felt lower than ever. "I'm going out for a walk," I said to Ruth.

It was raining now, but I didn't care. At first I went around the block a few times, and then down farther toward my parents' house, but I didn't go there. I walked past, toward the center of town, kind of circling in ever smaller squares, moving in on something as slowly as I could, narrowing in toward some point, not even knowing what it was, and wanting to take as long as possible to get there.

Finally I was there. And then I knew. It was the address—a pool hall where the two promoters hung out.

I walked in, saw one of them, went up to him.

"I'll run against your horses," I half-whispered.

"Dark lowers the tempest overhead,
The roaring torrent is deep and wide!"

CHAPTER NINE

Dear Luz,

I got your letter, and it was great to hear from you. I would have written before this, but things haven't been going my way since Berlin, and I was waiting until I could tell you something good.

Yet I don't want too much time to pass, so I'll just tell you what's going on now and hope that by the next time I write, things will have worked out. I'm sure they will.

What I've got to do in a couple of days is run a race against a—

I began to write the words race horse, but I couldn't. It was at least the tenth time I'd crumpled up a letter to Luz that I'd begun and thrown it in the wastebasket.

He was the one who would understand more than anyone else how it hurt me to have to do what I was going to do Friday night. And yet somehow, I couldn't tell him. Couldn't tell anybody what I really felt.

Ruth knew, of course. My parents sensed it. But no one said anything to me. Still—was it any worse than sharecropping?

I found out that Friday night.

It was worse than sharecropping.

It was bad enough to have toppled from the Olympic heights to make my living competing with animals. But the competition wasn't even fair. No man could beat a race horse, not even for 100 yards.

Unless the race began on the man's terms, by the shooting off of a gun. A gun held very close to the horse's head. That would make the animal rear up for an instant, and take another second to come down and get into stride. Oh, that horse would be moving like a railroad train at the finish line, but it would be too late. The man—if he were the world's fastest human, anyway—would beat the horse by a handful of yards.

It made me sick. But I did it. Why did I do it? To survive—no, because I thought I had to do it in order to survive.

Even then, I couldn't do it for that long. One Saturday night, when we were in Canton only sixty miles from home, I went to see one of the promoters about an hour before the baseball game, and a half-hour before my race.

"I can't do it tonight," I told him. "Or any night."

"What are you talking about?"

"I'm sorry not to be able to tell you more in advance. I knew it was coming on, but I didn't know it would get to me all at once. Anyway, I can't do it again. I can't race that horse again."

"You won't get your money for the week."

It was the first time I'd laughed since I started this thing. "You keep it," I told him, and walked out.

It had been good money. There'd been enough to get a little ahead again on my parents' house, support Ruth and my daughter and now the new baby, but where did I go from here?

My mother's proverb came true again. Just as I was about to go back to my job as Cleveland playground instructor, another pair of promoters appeared at my apartment. They weren't asking me to race against any horses, thank God. They weren't asking me to use my body at all—they wanted me to use my mind. Or so they said. They had an idea for a chain of cleaning stores, "The Jesse Owens Cleaners."

I grabbed at it like you grab the baton in a relay race from a man who's almost out of the legal passing zone—just in time.

And this time, it seemed like I was on top again. All my life had been such extremes—either the lowest or the highest, with nothing in between—and whenever something seemed to be going good, it was natural to think it would turn out to be another 1936 Olympics.

For openers, the money rolled in. My partners paid me on time, and a lot. I paid off the entire mortgage on my parents' house: I'd never have to worry about that again.

Ruth and I and the girls moved into a house of our own. That I would have to worry about, but there didn't seem to be any cause. The cleaning store turned into two, two into six, six into more than a dozen, and it looked like there was no end in sight. From that first trip we took to Cleveland north from Oakville, I always loved to travel and it would be a great kick for Ruth and I to go from town to town, seeing the new Jesse Owens Cleaners.

There was only one nagging feeling: I wasn't really using my mind to make the cleaning stores a success. I was actually only putting my name on them. I kept asking for more responsibility, even insisting on it, but since I didn't know what there was to be done, all that happened was that they gave me something new to do which any smart clerk could have done.

One morning at breakfast, Ruth and I really talked it out. "We're making money, but you're not doing anything with your life, Jesse," she finally said. "You've got to go to those men and either become a real part of it, as you would be on a relay team, or have them buy you out." I knew she was right. I'd been thinking the same thing myself for weeks.

I gave one of the investors a call, but no one answered. I called his partner—my partner—and no one answered. So I went on down to the main cleaning store. Somebody would know something.

When I got there, only a skeleton crew was around. "Anybody know where I can find Nat? Or Jack?" I asked. But I didn't have much hope for a definite answer. These people were only the clerks and no one did know.

"How come no one else is here?" I asked.

Again, no one knew. They only knew that they were told to stay on if the others didn't show up. I went out and called Jack and Nat again. Nothing. I drove several miles to the next store. Another skeleton crew. And no information. I drove to the next town. This time, there wasn't even a skeleton crew. There was only a sign on the door. TEMPORARILY CLOSED. I hurried back to Cleveland, fear fisting inside my stomach. I kept fighting it down, but it kept getting hold of my insides again and again—the same kind of fear, I knew, that my father had felt every winter when Mr. Clannon counted up the money and figured out daddy's share.

I tried everything I could think of to reach my two partners that night, but they were nowhere to be found. I never saw either of them again, in fact. But the next morning, a man serving legal papers found me when I went back to the main store.

It turned out that the two men who had put me in business had also put the three of us in bankruptcy except that there was only one of us left to pay for it. They'd used my name to gain loans for the stores, paid me well so I wouldn't be suspicious, but slowly, surely had gotten behind paying everyone else, from rents that were due to employees who had believed nothing could go wrong because they worked for the Jesse Owens Cleaners to firms that supplied equipment. And, last but not least, the banks that held the notes for the loans.

I'd paid off my parents' house. I'd been able to go

back and finish my last year of college. I had bought Ruth some of the things she deserved, given my children some of the good things in life for the first time, too, even helped out my brothers and sisters.

And now, it seemed, I was beyond help. For this made almost not qualifying for the Olympics, or having to take a job as a playground instructor, or even racing against animals, seem like kid stuff.

Only having my blood unceasingly pouring out of me was like this.

I owed $114,000.

How could I ever hope to pay it back? And if I didn't, what would they do to me?

The total mountain of debt took the entire afternoon to unfold. When I walked into our living room that night, it was even more impossible to tell Ruth than it was to pay back the money. She already strongly suspected something was terribly wrong, though, from what had gone on the day before. I tried to break it to her a chunk at a time, but there was no way. It was a $114,000 mountain, and after about fifteen minutes, I had to let it fall on her, too. At that moment I would have given both my legs—the legs that gave me those four Olympic gold medals above the mantel in the living room—not to have had to tell Ruth Owens that her husband was more than a tenth of a million dollars in debt.

She didn't say anything, just sat still for what seemed like the longest time, and then began weeping softly. I put my arm around her, but there was nothing that I could say either. We stayed like that for I don't know how long, then I noticed she'd stopped weeping. I couldn't even cry. All I could think of was: *How am I going to pay back $114,000?* Even though I was still obsessed with the same thought a few minutes later when she came back to me, after gently disengaging herself and telling me she'd only be gone a minute, I suddenly said: "It'll be all right, Baby." It was the last thing in the world I felt, but I said it. Then I started crying. How was it going to be all right?

We got through the night somehow, kissed the children and put them to bed, then found ourselves alone together again in the front room. I took her hand, squeezed it, and we stayed like that, sitting for hours in stunned silence. Eventually, again, she excused herself to go into the other room, saying she'd be right back.

"It's okay, Baby," I whispered. "I want to take a walk anyway."

I knew why she was going in the other room, and why she had gone in there before.

To pray.

It touched me, deep, that she was doing that. But I didn't do it. Because what would I pray for?

To overcome a life-threatening illness so that I would grow up strong and healthy?

To leave the hard cotton fields of Alabama to come north and miraculously wind up with a college degree?

To go to a history-making Olympiad and find a unique friend who would sacrifice being in the limelight of the entire world for the sake of simply lending a helping human hand so that I could wind up with four gold medals and world records?

To ride through the streets of New York with countless people cheering me and have thousands of dollars in a brown bag thrown into my lap?

All my prayers had been answered.

And here I was.

I wrote a note to Ruth, left it by our bedroom door. It said not to worry, that I had to think things out. Then I locked the front door behind me, and started walking.

I walked and walked and walked, with no place to go. Eventually, I passed the pool hall where the baseball promoters hung out. An hour later, I passed by one of the Jesse Owens Cleaners. It was dark because this was the middle of the night, but tomorrow morning it would be dark in there too. I passed the playground, where I had taught youngsters how to run and jump. No longer could I go back to that.

I walked and I walked. I walked until I got lost, even in this city I'd come to know so well. I passed little streets I'd never seen, with rows of houses and apartments, a few of them with lights still burning. Were there happy people in those houses? Poor, exhausted, but happy?

I walked on. The night seemed to get blacker. Sometimes it was hard to see just where to go amid the dimly lit streets, but I kept on, doing the only thing I'd ever really known, moving, seeking.

Seeking an answer.

Hours passed. My legs were growing tired now, perspiration had soaked through all my clothing. But I didn't want to stop. I couldn't stop. Where was I going?

I was lost, but I knew that if I kept walking, I would come to something familiar. I wasn't afraid of being lost, only of not finding an answer. I walked on and on. Suddenly, I found it easier to make my way. It was because the sky now, ever so slowly but surely, was turning from black to a muted but phosphorescent red. In the east—and I knew it was east because of that—a fine line of light crimson rose just above the land, wherever there was a break in the buildings. I followed it, moved toward it, wanting to get closer, as if one could ever reach the horizon. But it seemed that I was, as the moments passed and my steps quickened and the muted crimson became filled with a brighter and brighter yellow. I began running, faster, the luminescence of the dawn that was sure to come making my own steps more and more sure, faster, stronger. I picked up speed, running through the predawn Cleveland streets almost as I ran on the field. Faster. Harder. Faster. Harder. Must get there. Must get where? Where?

All at once everything became familiar. I knew where I had been going all night. I slowed down, walked the last few yards.

I was home.

My father's home.

He was outside, waiting for me on the steps, smoking what seemed like the same pipe he'd always smoked way back in Oakville.

"Hello, J.C.," he said. "I knowed you was on your way."

And loud that clarion voice replied,
Excelsior!

CHAPTER TEN

Now I was walking again, only this time with my father.

The sun was coming up, the streets were beginning to busy themselves with those who had to rise with the sun to make a living. It reminded me that I had risen with the dawn all of my years, from Oakville to running before school for Charles Riley, to holding three jobs in college and training for the Olympics. Even when I was playground instructor, I was getting up before dawn each morning and buying the paper as soon as it came out to look for something better. It was only when I fell in with the promoters that I began sleeping later for the first time in my life. And it never felt natural. The first few days I took the job racing against the horses, I'd awaken early just out of habit, raring to go, even made breakfast for Ruth and the girls, worked out, took a shower, and answered some mail all before eight. Then I went on down to the promoters' offices. No one was in. So I jogged on over to the pool hall where they said they might be, but it wasn't open either. I found a little coffee shop next door, and had myself a glass of orange juice. In those days, it was always from fresh oranges. They squeezed it right in front of you, and you had seeds in your glass, had to be careful that you didn't drink them down. Not that it would have hurt you that much. I went on back to their offices then, but only a sleepy-eyed secretary had straggled in. She told me neither one of them usually arrived before two in the afternoon. After a few days, knowing there was nothing for me to do in the morning, I gradually began waking up later and later.

Something inside me now told me I'd never sleep late again. Part of me was wed to the land, and the land begins just before the dawn. Yet even if I worked twenty-three hours a day and slept only one, how would that make even a single dent in the mountain of debt under which I felt I was being buried?

That was what I asked my father when we finally got back to the house.

Not that there weren't sophisticated legal methods by which someone might be able to weasel out. But even if you did, you'd never come out of it with a good name. And with a good feeling inside you.

My father felt the same, felt even more strongly than I did. But he just said, "I don't know," when it came to how? "Let's have some vittles with momma," he said, "and then think on it some more. There's an answer somewhere, J.C."

I called Ruth from the other room and told her where I was. My mother fixed us a breakfast like in the old days, and in spite of the terrible troubles, just being there with the two of them, and I guess having walked all night, too, made me eat pretty good. My mother knew something was going on, but this was one of those times when, without saying anything, my father let her know it was between him and me. We took our coffee out on the porch then, while my mother cleaned up. She was humming. Nothing could stop that woman. I'd always been that way. Until now?

My father took a swallow of his coffee, then lit his pipe. A couple of hours ago when I told him how much I owed, he'd come as close to passing out as I'd ever seen, even including that day when we decided to leave Oakville. To him, there was hardly that much money in the world, let alone one person owing it! But as with everything else, he took it without breaking down, made peace with it, and now was trying to take it apart so that somehow it could be solved. He talked about selling the house, and about all my brothers and sisters pitching in and giving me and Ruth some of what they made year after year till it was all paid off.

I jumped up when he said that. "Daddy, then I'd owe all of you forever," I said. "I wouldn't be out of debt at all. And what I owed would be a worse burden, if that's possible."

He understood, much as he wanted me to go along. We just sat there then, not saying anything, my father thinking what other answer there could be, while I was becoming more and more worried about whether there could be any answer at all.

Eventually, he sat up. The years had bent him a little, but now he seemed to be straighter, almost as tall as I was. "Let's take another walk," he said. "To the church. We thought on it and we didn't figger out anything. So now we'll pray on it."

The little church he and my mother attended was the better part of two miles away. When we entered, no one else was inside. There was an unobtrusive collection box off to one side, and my father walked over and put a little change in it. I reached in my pocket, but I didn't have any coins. I hesitated for a second, then opened my wallet. There was only a single dollar. I hesitated again, then stuffed it into the box.

I followed him as he walked down the aisle, stopping a few rows in. He never had to be near the front. It was his way of saying that you got close to God from the inside, not the outside.

We knelt. Baptists seldom kneel, but this went deeper than denomination. And we prayed.

Just like we had in Oakville, Alabama, twenty-two years before when my blood was pouring out. My father and I prayed together.

Before we left the church, he stopped near the collection box. Just stared at it. He took out his pipe, put it in his mouth, but didn't light it. He was thinking hard about something.

"James Cleveland," he said when we were outside, grasping my arm emotionally, "that little box is the answer."

"You're not saying I should—"

He shook his head hard. "Pass around the hat? My son!" Then he smiled a little. "I meant something else, J.C. I was meaning . . . how much did you put into that box?"

I shrugged my shoulders a little. "A dollar."

He squeezed my arm again. "No, I mean how much of what you had?"

I was confused for a second. "Well, that's all I had on me—"

"Say it again!" He almost did a little dance.

"It's all—"

"Do you know what you're sayin', J.C.? That's the answer! You put everything you had into that box."

I looked at him, didn't say anything.

"Don't you see, J.C.? Don't you remember what one of momma's most favorite sayings is? What you puts in zackly is—"

"Exactly what you get out," I finished.

He nodded.

"But, Daddy, how'll I ever get $114,000 to put in?"

He put his arm around me, and we started walking faster. "Don't worry on that," he said. "Let's get home right now and you'll put the figures down on the paper, like you know how to do. I know it'll work. I knew it when I saw that box when we were leaving the church, and remembered how you put your last dollar in. Did you ever think you'd get to the Olympics? Or to *kolledge* when you were in Oakville? You got there because you put everything in it! You'll always be J.C. to me, and I'm never going to call you Jesse again. But you made a good name out of Jesse Owens, and a good name is hard to come by in this world. It's worth mor'n all the money you could ever make. Remember Mr. Clannon?" My father was talking as much as I'd ever heard him talk. Even when we used to walk home from church in Oakville. "He had a lot of money and a lot of things that he bought with it, but he didn't have no good name, did he? It don't profit a man none if he gits the whole world but loses what's inside himself. Let's git on home now!"

Ninety-nine per cent of me kept saying that he didn't know what he was talking about, that he didn't understand that no matter what figures we put down on paper, it wasn't going to add up to $114,000. But there was one small part of me, at the very bottom, that believed in him, and which couldn't be shaken by the mountain of so-called facts. He'd saved my life, hadn't he?

We got home, and I took pencil and paper and we kept talking about it, and writing down whatever we came up with. After a while, a long while, his "answer" emerged. I was twenty-seven years old, and I had at least forty-three good working years ahead of me. That meant, besides supporting my family, I had to come up with a little over $2,650 a year, or something over $50 a week, extra.

"You can do that if you holds two jobs," my father told me.

I was still almost speechless. "I guess I could," I said, "but it's fifty years you're talking about. It's my whole lifetime!"

"If it is, J.C.," he said soberly, "better to end up not owin' any man. And," he added softly, "you got a better way?"

There was no other way. I saw that. But I still saw how impossible the whole thing probably would be.

"Look, Daddy," I said, "let's say you're right. Let's say it's the only way. Let's say I want to do it. Do you think those banks that I owe the money to are going to wait fifty years?"

"I believe they might."

"Daddy, you sound like you're talking in tongues."

"I've knowed a lot of sense to be said in tongues."

"There's only one chance in a million."

"That's all you need, J.C. C'mon, boy, I'll go down to the bank with you."

So my father got dressed in his Sunday best, and we drove back to my house, and I got on my church suit, too, and I told Ruth that my father thought there might be an answer and we were going down to the bank to see.

I would honestly rather have sharecropped for Mr. Clannon than walk through the doors of that bank that afternoon. But in we went.

It took awhile before the right man sat down with us, but not that long. After all, I owed over $100,000. "I want to pay you what I owe you," I told him after we had introduced ourselves and shaken hands.

"What do you have in mind?" Mr. Melville asked.

I told him. It took everything I had to say it. Would he think I was a fool? Would he get angry and tell me to get out or even call the police? And would I blame him if he did?

He listened without saying anything until I'd outlined the whole incredible plan. He was silent for still another minute or two. It felt like a year or two. Strangely, then, he turned to my father. "And what do you think of this, Mr. Owens?"

My father held out his hands in an honest gesture. "It's the only way, isn't it?"

The banker looked back at me. "You'll have to excuse me for a little while. I have to call a couple of people before I can give you an answer."

Again, we waited. And waited. After forty-five minutes, he returned.

"All right, Jesse," he said, looking at both of us really, "we've decided to accept your offer."

I was thunderstruck!

"There'll be a few papers to sign, and a little bit of interest, though we'll keep it as low as possible," he went on. "We'll have them ready for you by the end of the week."

My father looked at me and smiled. Then he started to get up, and offered his hand to the banker. "Thank you, sir," he said.

"Yes, thank you," I said and shook hands with him, yet not with my usual grip. And I couldn't get up out of the chair. I tried, but so help me, I couldn't.

"Well, gentlemen," the man said, "I guess that about does it. Why don't you call me tomorrow and I'll let you know exactly what day to come in."

I still sat there, dumbfounded. He looked at me with questioning eyes. "Is there something else, Jesse?"

"Yes," I stammered. "Why . . . why are you doing this . . . trusting me?"

He thought for a few seconds before answering, as if he knew the answer, but didn't know quite how he wanted to say it, or whether he wanted to say it at all. "People think of bankers as cold and inhuman," he finally answered. "But the main part of our business is lending money to people. It all comes down to whether they're honest or not, whether they'll pay it back. So it's a very human business, and we wouldn't last very long if we didn't choose the right people. So what matters most is not how long you'll take, or how hard it is, but how good a bet you are to pay it back. We think you're a very good bet."

Then I was able to stand up. I actually wanted to come around the desk and throw my arms around him. Instead, I tried to say it with my expression. My father and I turned to leave.

"Jesse—" he said.

My daddy and I turned.

"There's one more thing," he almost whispered. "I'm half Jewish." Now his voice was a whisper. "There are very few Jewish people who can get along in banking. Even less who can get along in Germany today." He paused one more time. "How could I ever not trust the man who beat Hitler?"

I was so moved that I half-stammered out my words. "Thanks . . . but Hitler isn't beaten yet."

Mr. Melville's face grew grim. "I know," he said. "But he must be beaten. The unfree, the unbelieving—which is really what makes Hitler

113

possible, isn't it?—has to be beaten."

My father hadn't said anything for a long time. Now, he stepped forward a little bit. He waited until he was sure that neither Mr. Melville nor myself were going to speak.

"One thing," my daddy said in the most serene voice I have ever heard.

Mr. Melville and I both turned to him, our eyes questioning.

"We've got Someone on our side that Mr. Hitler doesn't."

"Oh, stay," the maiden said, "and rest
Thy weary head upon this breast!"

CHAPTER ELEVEN

Little did I dream how prophetic my father's words would be.

Little did I dream that soon again I would be locked in an even more crucial confrontation with Hitler.

As every school child knows, the Nazi dictator made war not only on Europe, but on the world. On December 7, 1941, my own beloved America finally was forced to fight for the freedoms we'd always taken for granted. I guess we all knew it was coming, though we didn't want to face it until there was no turning away.

For most Americans, that came on December 7, 1941.

For me, it came on September 25, 1940.

Though I had found it hard sometimes to write Luz throughout my financial crises, I would always get at least a half page letter off to him whenever three or four months had passed. He always wrote back promptly, or even wrote his next letter without my answering his last one.

But then, the letters stopped.

Three or four months passed without his writing me. Then another three or four. It was by far the greatest amount of time which had ever passed without my getting a letter from Luz. I wrote him. I waited. Nothing. I wrote him again. Nothing. Then again—just a note asking for him to answer, to let me know he was all right, nothing more.

But no answer arrived.

A year had passed now. Then more. One year became two. I knew that Germany was already at war with the rest of Europe. I knew that Luz, incredible athlete that he was, would be in the thick of it. I feared for him, even woke up in the middle of the night more than once, a nightmare about him blotting out all my own personal nightmares. So, each day, each week, each month that the reports on the radio and the stories in the newspapers about Hilter's advances grew malignantly bigger and bolder, I grew more fearful for Luz Long. More than once, I prayed that the war would end, not only to save so many lives and so much destruction, but to save his life. Yet in my heart, I sensed that Luz's life had already been taken.

Then one day, a letter arrived!

I was so joyful to receive it, that it took a moment before the date in the corner got through to me. The letter was well over a year old. It was from the North

African desert. It read:

I am here, Jesse, where it seems there is only the dry sand and the wet blood. I do not fear so much for myself, my friend Jesse, I fear for my woman who is home, and my young son Karl, who has never really known his father.

My heart tells me, if I be honest with you, that this is the last letter I shall ever write. If it is so, I ask you something. It is a something so very important to me. It is you to go to Germany when this war is done, someday find my Karl, and tell him about his father. Tell him, Jesse, what times were like when we not separated by war. I am saying—tell him how things can be between men on this earth.

If you do this something for me, this thing that I need the most to know will be done, I do something for you, now. I tell you something I know you want to hear. And it is true.

That hour in Berlin when I first spoke to you, when you had your knee upon the ground, I knew that you were in prayer.

Then I not know how I know. Now I do. I know it is never by chance that we come together. I come to you that hour in 1936 for purpose more than der Berliner Olympiade.

And you, I believe, will read this letter, while it should not be possible to reach you ever, for purpose more even than our friendship.

I believe this shall come about because I think now that God will make it come about.

This is what I have to tell you, Jesse.

I think I might believe in God.

And I pray to him that, even while it should not be possible for this to reach you ever, these words I write will still be read by you.

Your brother,

Luz

That moment, I felt not only that Luz was my brother, but closer to me in a way than even my own kin.

And I sensed that he was the one brother I would never see again even though we'd vowed to meet at least one more time.

Yet I was moved, almost shocked, by his telling me that he had begun to believe in God. But how could it be God's plan that Luz should die because of a madman like Hitler? Still, the loss of Luz was not as great as two other losses I was soon to suffer.

They had nothing to do with money—that began to go well. I steered a straight and narrow course, finding whatever work I could, holding two jobs at once, but still somehow gaining precious time for Ruth and the three girls, and day by day, dollar by dollar, the huge debt almost invisibly, but surely, grew smaller. I made the payments weekly instead of monthly, sometimes even going in twice a week if I'd somehow gotten some extra money. I always paid on time, often paying more. I didn't want it to take fifty years.

When World War II broke out that Sunday night in 1941, I got on the phone and called one of the fellows who had been on the Olympic squad with me. He was now a lieutenant in the army. I told him I wanted to do my part. He said he understood, and would call me the following day.

When the phone rang at two-thirty the following afternoon—I had taken the first day away from work in almost two years—it turned out to be someone higher up in the government, who my pal had spoken to. He said he had something that no one else could do which he and someone in President Roosevelt's cabinet wanted me to take a crack at. He told me that travel arrangements had already been made, and he'd like to see me in Washington, D.C. the following day. When I reached Washington, I was taken into an office in the White House itself.

And there, I met the President of the United States.

"Jesse Owens," he said, "we're in a terrible war, one that will not be easy to win. I think you can help us to move toward victory."

I had gooseflesh. I shook hands with President Roosevelt—he was the first of four presidents whose hands I would shake, though I never dreamed that at the time—and went into another room where I was briefed by the man I'd talked to on the phone and several others. What they wanted me to do was to supervise the hiring of Negroes for the wartime effort in the Ford Motor Plant in Detroit.

It was a big job.

It also turned out to be a rewarding one. Not many Negroes had been hired for jobs in the auto plants before that, and it was up to me to pick the right ones, not only so they'd get along with the whites, but so that we'd all get the job done and win the war.

It was rewarding in another way. I was paid well, and could see that within a few years, if I scrimped and saved every penny of what I made, I might be totally out of debt. As it turned out, the Friday before the Germans surrendered, I made my final payment.

But two infinitely more important final payments had been made in the year before that.

First, my mother died.

It was sudden, and I didn't expect it. None of us did.

How could my mother die? She was so indomitable—nothing had ever stopped her. We didn't have any older relatives up in Cleveland, so I'd never really known death until then. Yes, I'd heard of the children my momma had lost before she had me, but I'd never really known anyone I loved to die.

Suddenly, one morning, my mother was gone. Her heart had stopped beating in the middle of the night. She had turned to my father, held him with tiny hands of iron. Yet, when her grip had loosened, she was gone.

I couldn't believe it. She was the kind of person who seemed like she'd never die. Maybe there was a chance Luz was alive, but if he was gone, much as I'd feel his loss forever, I'd understand it. Fighting in a war like that.

But . . . my mother.

I couldn't accept it, but finally I believed it. Seeing is believing. I knew that if there was a better place than this earth, she was there. But I wanted her here! I cried like a baby, off and on, for three days after the funeral.

Yet finally, I dried my tears. I still had my father. I had loved my mother—did love her—because she was part of me. And because she was my momma. I think I loved her, if I dare say this, as much as any son loved his mother.

And it wasn't that I loved my daddy more. It was that I loved him different.

After my mother was gone, I got scared. I didn't want to lose my father. It was as if my mother was still alive, because she was part of me, I was more like her. But my daddy—he was something different, something I didn't have inside myself for certain, something I needed.

I tried to comfort him, tried like I'd never tried before. But I knew deep in my heart, because she was no longer with him, that he wanted to go wherever she had gone.

Seven months later, he did.

With him, it was sudden too—yet not all at once. I called the doctor, but all he did was make my father a little more comfortable. "There's nothing I can do," he said.

"There's got to be," I told him.

He just looked at me, put a comforting hand on mine, and turned slowly to go.

I'd save my father, then!

I couldn't let him die.

My brothers and sisters were there, and the older grandchildren. All the chairs were taken. Ruth was sitting on one edge of the bed, my sister on the other. I found room by kneeling near where my father's head was propped up on the pillow.

"Don't give in, Daddy . . . don't give in to it. . . ."

He turned his eyes, but not his head. "J.C.," was all he said. His heart was so weak. It was my mother's brain, her will, that had given out. It was my father's heart, his soul.

He closed his eyes. I felt fear as I'd never known grip my own heart like a vise. Was he going to die? All I could do was wait.

I waited.

I don't know how many hours passed. One by one, the others would come in and go out, keeping the vigil. I never left. It was that hour before dawn, that hour when it's blackest, when I realized I was alone with him for the first time. The others were either sleeping, or in the other room.

He opened his eyes. "I'm goin' . . . with your momma . . . now . . . J.C. . . . ," he whispered.

"No, Daddy, you can't."

I think his lips moved ever so slightly in what might have been a smile. Or maybe he was going to say something. But he didn't.

I spoke. "Please, Daddy, please. Stay with me. Stay with me awhile longer, at least. Please—"

His eyes answered.

He was going to die. He was ready to die, and there was nothing I could do to change it.

I prayed.

I prayed for him to live.

But I knew that my prayers wouldn't change it, either.

"Daddy," I pleaded. "I don't even know how to pray without you. Tell me how to pray, Daddy. Like that time we did in Oakville. When you saved my life. How did we pray then? How? Tell me how, please tell me how, Daddy!"

Suddenly, I was quiet. I sensed something, and though I'd been babbling like a child, all at once I stopped speaking. I knew my father was trying to speak. He was trying to tell me something.

More time passed. I could see him straining—and I didn't want him to, but I wanted him to tell me—and then, finally, the sounds choked out.

But they were only sounds, not words.

And when they were no more, my father's heartbeat was no more.

A tear stood in his bright blue eye. . . .

CHAPTER TWELVE

What had my father wanted to tell me?

I thought of almost nothing else—when I wasn't buried in grief—in the weeks that followed. But I couldn't find a clue. It was as if I could bring my father back if I discovered what he wanted to say to me at the end. In my mind, it would be as if he was still speaking to me.

Yet I couldn't. So, almost without realizing what I was doing, I turned to finding out whether Luz's final sentences to me were his last words.

Though I'd moved on to even better work, and begun speaking before groups for some pretty impressive fees, I knew some key people in Washington because of my wartime work. They set the wheels in motion, and those wheels churned like a champion hurdler's legs as I called, sometimes two or three and four times a day, to see if they'd found out anything. It became an obsession. I didn't see that what I really wanted to know was that something so profoundly important which my father had always known.

But the day came when I could no longer replace finding out my father's final words with learning Luz's last words.

Because his last words were to me, just as my father's had been. I learned that Luz had been killed in that North African desert a day or two after he wrote me.

My beloved friend's last lines spoke of God, my beloved father's final sounds were of prayer, but neither held the answer I was seeking.

Again, without really realizing what I was doing, I replaced the quest for one answer with the search for another. From my inward struggles, I turned to an outward struggle—one I was more familiar with, one to which, no matter how difficult the struggle became, I always seemed to have a final answer.

The struggle within the world.

My debt was paid, but I worked as few men ever have. People who worked with me or knew me still called me "the world's fastest human" because I almost never stopped. I'd found that I could get more done with no regular job or regular hours at all, but by being on my own, flying to speak here, help with a public relations campaign for some client there, tape my regular jazz radio show one morning at 5:00 A.M. before leaving on a plane for another city or another continent three hours later to preside over a major sporting event. I moved my family to Chicago, because I thought it would be a better place for Ruth and the girls, but I was with them less and less now. I recall one time—though there were many just like this—when after being gone for more than a week, I arrived back and Ruth picked me up at the airport. I told her that I would have to fly out again six hours later, but at least we could all have dinner together.

We got back to the apartment and waited for the girls to come home from school. Ruth and I sat down in the den. But I kept getting up out of my chair, walking around the room, like an animal in a cage. Ruth, who hardly ever criticizes directly, eventually stood up, took both my hands in hers as if to hold me still.

"Jesse," she said. "Can't you even sit still for five minutes? Can't you even sit in a chair for 300 seconds?"

I sat down, then. But after a few minutes, it was true, I did feel like getting up again and moving. Three hundred seconds. You could run thirty 100-meter dashes in that time—if you broke the world's record.

The world's record. Incredibly, after all these years, mine were still standing. Athletes were getting bigger and stronger and faster, training methods and equipment had improved immeasurably. But my running and jumping records were still intact. In fact, when it came to leaping into the air and seeing how far you could go before you came down, no one had even come close—not since Luz Long.

I thought of Luz, but less and less. I thought of my father and mother, but less and less. The pain was always there when I did think about them, the pain never became less, but now I didn't have it as often.

One of my brothers died. One of my sisters. Each cut through to my very center, made me feel the other deaths almost as if they had just happened. But now, afterward, I no longer sat alone and sought answers from within. I had a plane to catch. I had just been appointed top public relations representative for one of the country's largest firms. A huge Hollywood studio phoned about doing a story of my life. President Eisenhower sent me a telegram, asking me to fly to Washington so that he could make me special ambassador for my country in every non-Communist nation on earth, teaching youngsters how to run and jump, and about the American way of life.

But what of my own children? What of my own way of life?

I was gone from home for longer and longer periods now. Two weeks. Three weeks. Then, when I went on a major junket for the President—trying somehow to work in my other activities by flying in and out of foreign cities at all hours of the day and night—for more than a month.

I wasn't blind, I knew what was happening. But things were moving so fast. Months became years before I could catch my breath. Sure, there were times when I tried to put aside a week, but that was almost impossible. So then I attempted to carve out long weekends, but they were always suddenly shortened by one commitment leading to another. I was making a great deal of money, but I was spending a great deal of money. One way to cut through the painful periods of absence, I thought, to reestablish the intimacy at once, was to walk in with diamond bracelets for Ruth and exotic dolls for the girls from foreign lands.

But intimacy takes time. And my time had been spent in making the money that I spent to try to regain the intimacy I'd once known with my family without the money.

I saw it happening. I saw it happening and I struggled to change it, to break the bonds that held me away from home week after week, month after month, and reunite the bonds with the four human beings on earth who mattered most to me. Like a man caught in quicksand, the harder I struggled, the deeper I sank.

And more time passed.

"I've got to be with you and the girls more," I told Ruth one Sunday night at the airport, my voice husky with emotion. I was about to leave for a three-week tour of the southeast part of the world.

"There must be a way," she answered.

"We've got to find it—and soon," I said, kissing her goodbye.

I began to cut the "after" part of speeches that I made, things that I did, to simply go back to my hotel room and think—think *how to do it*. I even turned down several lucrative offers, because it would have meant being away from Ruth and the girls on special occasions. But what about the special occasions that weren't "special"—the little, day-to-day things that turn out to be quite large in the end, the things that come from living with the people you love? Those I didn't have—those I didn't give—because I wasn't there. I couldn't turn down everything. I needed the money. Times had changed, it cost more to live, and to be brutally honest, I wanted Ruth and the girls to live well. I never wanted to go back to being that Alabama sharecropper's starving son. I never wanted my daughters to have any idea of what that was like.

And time marched on.

If I was no longer the starving sharecropper's son, neither was I the boy growing up in Cleveland, the world-famous Olympic athlete, or even the former Olympic immortal struggling to make a living in a world new to him. If I was no longer the starving five-year-old boy in Oakville, neither was I the fifteen-year-old schoolboy, the twenty-three-year-old champion, the thirty-two-year-old businessman.

I was middle-aged.

My wife, though still youthfully beautiful, was middle-aged.

My girls were becoming women.

It all seemed to come crashing through to me once and for all on a Tuesday in September of 1956. The next day was to be my forty-third birthday. Ruth had talked for months about my putting aside time, because she and the girls had not celebrated one of my birthdays with me for years now.

This time, as always, though I tried to keep a couple of days open on both sides, just to make sure, stone by stone, the two walls I had built—one two days before September 12th, the other two days after—began to crumble. The Boy Scouts wanted just an hour of my time only 150 miles from where I'd be on September 14. So if I could leave the night before instead of the following morning . . . and a church group in Indianapolis where I was going to speak on the 10th, asked if I could stay over that night because of some crippled children—

And so the walls crumbled.

I wired one civic organization to say that I regretfully couldn't accept the award they wanted to give me because of personal matters at home, moved back another commitment a week, promising an extra half-day to them. Still, it didn't leave much.

I arrived home, breathlessly, on a Tuesday night. *I'll be there in time to kiss the little one goodnight before she goes to sleep,* I thought to myself.

But the little one was no longer little. It's strange, and so sad, how you can fix on something in your mind, attach yourself to a stage of life that was, and blind yourself to the truth that one stage becomes another as quietly but as certainly as the ice breaks away from spring ponds and becomes vibrantly flowing, warm summer streams. Oh, you always think of your children as children, but this was more than that. I really hadn't been there as they had grown up. Too often, I had missed the bittersweet miracle of watching them grow.

That night, not only was my baby, Marlene, too old to be told any bedtime stories by her father, because she had an important date, but Gloria, my oldest, though she had bought me a beautiful gift and was looking forward to the birthday celebration the next day, had to rush out for a civil rights meeting, which she was into long before it was fashionable. Yet Beverly, my middle one, was at home. After kissing me hello, she went back in her room. It was unusual for her. In personality, Beverly was more like me than Marlene or Gloria—she was outgoing, impulsive.

Ruth took me aside. "Jesse, there's something Beverly wanted me to discuss with you."

"What's that, Baby?"

Ruth motioned me to sit down, but I've always been more comfortable standing than sitting. She paused for a second, as if she was taking a deep breath—though why would she do that?—and then she said simply, "Beverly wants to get married, Jesse."

I sat down.

"But she can't!" I said. "She's too young. Way too young—"

Ruth smiled. "Look who's talkin'," she kidded.

Beverly had one other quality of mine in great abundance. She was headstrong. She came out of her room, and no matter what I said, though she showed her love for me, she made it quite clear that she was going to be married and that there was nothing anyone could do about it.

The next day we celebrated my birthday.

The following night, I left for still another city, still another state. I was to do the highlight commentary on a key outdoor track and field meet. Since the war ended, the United States seemed to have experienced an athletic boom. Sports like golf, tennis and bowling were growing fast. Football, baseball and basketball were about to expand, but maybe most of all, things were being done in track and field that had never been done before. One example was the oncoming reign of the fiberglass pole which lifted vaulters not just within inches of Cornelius Warmerdam's incredible 15 feet 8 inches, or inches past it, but whole *feet* further. The supposedly "impossible" 4-minute mile wouldn't even be a memory to the grandchildren I knew I was soon to have. And that night, something else was supposed to happen—a young sprinter looked like he had a good chance at cracking Jesse Owens' twenty-one-year-old 100-yard dash mark.

My job was to tell the world about it while he was breaking the record.

I was working with a famous announcer. I felt a peculiar tension that night, but I didn't let it show. Then it came time for the 100-yard dash. The other announcer and I discussed the different performers, then the one in particular who was almost a sure thing to win and a threat to my record. "What would you feel if he broke that record, Jesse?" my reporting partner asked me.

"It's nice that it lasted this long," I answered, with good fellowship in my voice, "but records are made to be broken—that's what human progress is all about—and if it has to be done tonight, this boy will make a fine new champion."

I said it, and part of me meant it. Part of me. But another part, and a larger one, didn't want him to break the record.

Maybe it was only natural, I told myself.

But it was more than just not wanting my record to be broken. It was that my 100-yard dash mark seemed connected to all kinds of other things—I didn't know what exactly—and if this boy wiped one of them from the books, he'd wipe them all away somehow.

I tried to put it out of my mind, but I couldn't as the race was about to begin. I gave a last comment or two, and it wasn't easy, and then the fellow I was working with took over. He was good. The 100-yard dash is a fast race, not like a horse race where you have a minute or two to spot your leaders and your challengers and the horses that are dropping back, make your calls and build the excitement. Here, you've got to get off with the gun just as the runner must, know who's in front—whether he's moving more in front—whether anybody has a chance of catching him in those last fifty yards which fly by in a literal handful of seconds!

"The gun!" he yelled into the microphone, almost before the sharp sound was heard in the air. "Morrow's out in front—got a great start. Ronnie's trying to run at him, cut down the lead but he can't— Bobby's pulling away—he's moving incredibly fast— he's hit the tape and I have an unofficial clocking of 9.2—hold on a minute—so does one timekeeper—now let's see what the other two have—if one of their watches agrees, tonight we'll have a new world's fastest human!"

The instant I heard those words, I felt a bolt of pain go through me, all the way down and in, and I literally doubled up. "What's wrong, Jesse?" the commentator whispered to me off-mike.

"Nothing . . . I'll be okay in a second or two," I whispered back. "I've had a thing with my stomach the last few months. . . ."

I straightened up, pain or no pain. In fact, I stood up. I thought it was an act of will, to prove to myself that I could take it. What I was really doing was rising on the witness stand, waiting for the verdict.

My record was not broken that night. Bobby missed by a tenth of a second. I was still "the world's fastest human," though my days were numbered. I got in my car and headed toward the airport, was supposed to be in San Francisco. I must have been about halfway when I passed what looked like a field, swung the car right into it, turned around and headed for home.

Instead of parking in our garage behind the apartment building, I took the first place I found several blocks away, then I began walking. There were people sitting out on their porches, and they waved to me. Kids who were playing out later than they should have been yelled, "Jesse Owens!" I waved back. I love kids.

I had stayed one, when you came right down to it, hadn't I?

The last block was only apartment buildings, and I was alone. As I passed under each street light, I noticed butterflies—those beautiful orange and black ones—lying dead at the edge of the small plots of grass. Most of them were upright, or at an angle, as if they were just resting and would fly away at any second. But they were dead. It was September, and every September I knew, particularly because it was the month of my birthday, things that only last one season begin to die.

Some lines from the Bible which my mother taught

me kept running through my mind. She always used to make us memorize a different passage every week, but sometimes she would forget and she would keep teaching us the ones she liked over and over throughout the years. This one was from Corinthians, and it might have been her favorite.

I opened the front door to our apartment. Ruth was alone there, startled to see me.

"I'm not taking the plane to San Francisco," I told her before she said anything. "I'm canceling out. I'm going to cancel a lot of things. It might take a few months—but I'm not going to let it take any longer—until I can be home most of the time like other men with my family."

She threw her arms around me and began sobbing.

That night after the girls came home and were all finally asleep, we made love, and Ruth then fell asleep cradled between my arm and my shoulder. I was at peace, but I didn't sleep for a long time. I thought about all the things I would have to do in order to center my activities in Chicago. I thought about some of the sacrifices that might have to be made. I thought about the beauty of being with my family which would be the reward. For the first time, really, I would be a full-time husband and father.

When I finally shut my eyes, those lines that my mother taught me echoed back again:

But when that which is perfect is come, then that which is in part shall be done away. When I was a child, I spake as a child, I understood as a child, I thought as a child: but when I became a man, I put away childish things. (1 Cor. 13:10-11)

But still he answered with a sigh,
Excelsior!

CHAPTER THIRTEEN

Now I was working twenty hours a day to make everything somehow center around my home. What I couldn't, I let go of as soon as I could afford to, building new things in Chicago to take their place. I knew it was the right thing to do, and I did it. Within less than six months, I was home a majority of the time. Within a few months after that, there were some periods when I was home virtually all the time. I bunched my international duties within a compass of a few weeks; I scheduled speaking appearances and youth clinics one right after the other, never being gone more than a handful of days at a time.

It wasn't an easy change, but one by one I found things in Chicago to make a living. Above all, I was making that living not five miles from where I lived, sometimes out of my own home!

And from that point on, everything went downhill for me.

For ten years, almost everything went bad until, finally, I was in a crisis that made $114,000 of debt, or even almost bleeding to death in Oakville, seem unimportant.

Why did it happen? I don't know. To this day, I don't know. I don't have all the answers.

Maybe it was because I had done the right thing at the wrong time—too late. Or maybe it was because, though I did it all the way in one way, I didn't sacrifice my high standard of living. I do know that everything we do sets invisible forces into motion, which come back to bless or haunt us at the strangest times.

Possibly it was simply that I was being tested. I certainly believe, as my father did, that life, whatever else it is for us, is a supreme test.

I don't know.

I only know what happened—without my wanting it to happen or doing anything to make it happen.

Possibly the most important activity I'd found in Chicago—really the one that shifted the balance so that home could become "home base"—was heading up the Juvenile Delinquency Prevention Program for the Illinois Youth Commission. Like any job with the state where you don't run for office, it took a political appointment, but I kind of thought I was above politics. I'd worked hard with those kids, bringing them along one by one, though there were thousands and thousands who themselves were hanging in the balance. They were mostly black, but there were some white ones too—all assortments, in fact. The way in which they were the same was more important than the ways in which they were different, as I've always found to be true of human beings anywhere. These kids, whether they were five-year-old near-dope addicts or fifteen-year-old near-hardened criminals, had the one thing in common of living in a moral ghetto the likes of which I had never seen on this earth, even in the most backward countries. It made me know how lucky I had been to be born into only Oakville's mere material deprivation.

On a Friday morning, after I'd been up till three in the morning the night before finding a runaway teen who I'd taken out of a juvenile home and gotten a job after school washing dishes and who'd split from fear of failure with the first dish he'd broken, I received a printed slip in my mailbox.

I had gotten Mark back his job as dishwasher. But I'd never be able to do it again. I'd lost my job.

That Monday, though, I wouldn't have been able to go to work for very long, anyway. I had to go to a funeral. The other main activity I'd built in Chicago was a small P.R. agency, just a handful of select clients with whom I could live—meaning say good things about them and mean those things. I'd found less than half a dozen clients I could do that with, but for them I was able to do a lot and they paid me well. That weekend, one of them died suddenly. He *was* his business, so that was lost for good. And, more important, a good friend was lost because that is what my handful of clients had become to me, and this man in particular.

One week later, another client was in a serious auto accident. He survived, but was forced into early retirement.

When I heard about the death, I felt dizzy and sick. When I heard about the accident, I doubled over in pain, as I had that night when my record was nearly broken. It had been broken since. All my records were gone, except for the jumping.

This time, though, the pain didn't subside—not for a few hours, at least. And I had other symptoms with it, soon afterward. Then a few days later, the pain came again, worse. I went to see a doctor and I was surprised—because I always thought, beneath it all, that sickness could never touch me—when he wanted to do a complete medical checkup, particularly x-rays on my gut. I wasn't going to, but Ruth felt so terrible about my not finding out what was wrong, that I gave in. It turned out that I had ulcers all over my intestines. Some people die of it, but I got it under control. In fact, I amazed the doctors—they said they'd never seen such a quick and what looked like complete recovery. But, just as quickly, almost as if there was some unlucky something inside me which had merely moved to another spot, I developed pneumonia.

At first, that's all it was. I took some shots, and the coughing seemed to subside. The time was coming up when I had to go out of town, so it was a good thing. Except that when my plane was halfway over the ocean, I began coughing again. By the time the plane landed, I had barely enough strength to board another plane back. I didn't go home—I went straight to the hospital.

And collapsed.

The lungs which had helped take me to four gold medals now were in danger of taking me from life. The pneumonia had returned, spreading to both lungs, and no drugs the doctors gave seemed to matter. For days, I lay in an oxygen tent, half-unconscious most of the time, my only real memory being that of seeing Ruth's face through the plastic-like material, always there, the love in her face and my own will to live, no matter what, set against the dour looks of the doctors. Not even the oxygen tent and the fact that they stood out in the hall could hide what was on their faces. They thought I was going to die.

But I didn't.

I got out of that bed, and I went home. I was weak for a couple of days, but then the energy came surging back, like always. I felt good. I felt like the worst was over. I had suffered some setbacks, sure, but wasn't it my father who always said that life was a test?

I worked my fanny off for the next week, got a lot done—began to build back some of the income that I'd lost. I accomplished so much, in fact, that I decided to give myself a rare reward. It had been months since I'd had time to play golf. I took a Saturday off, and went out to the public course—there were no clubs for Negroes—for a round.

It seemed like old times when I teed off at the first hole. One of my buddies said that he thought the ball actually went 300 yards, though I doubt whether it was that long a drive. The body doesn't forget, though, and I expected to shoot a darn good score that day.

Except that I never made it past the first hole.

On my second shot, a pain went through my back and down my leg that was like my mother's knife cutting the bump out of my body. It was so intense that I froze in shock. Then, gradually, the pain lessened, then let up even more, till there was no pain at all.

Because I couldn't feel.

I was paralyzed from the waist down.

*"Beware the pine tree's
withered branch!"*

CHAPTER FOURTEEN

There's a passage in that unforgettable film *Butch Cassidy and the Sundance Kid*, where Butch and Sundance are applying for a job in their attempt to leave behind a life of crime. The employer lets them know that whether they're hired will depend on how well Sundance can shoot. The prospective employer takes a small piece of wood and hurls it thirty yards away. "Can you hit that?" he says.

Sundance poises his hand over his holster as if to get ready to draw. "No, no," the older man says. "Just take out your gun and let's see if you can hit it."

So Sundance takes his gun, aims, and misses. The employer is obviously disappointed and not going to hire them.

"Can I move?" Sundance suddenly asks him.

"Move?" the employer exclaims. "What do you mean

move?"

Sundance then poises his hand over his holster again and in one motion pulls out the gun, jerking his body as he does it, shoots, and not only hits the wood, but splits it in half and then quarters when it is flying up in the air! The employer's eyes almost pop out of his head.

"I'm better when I move," Sundance says.

I've always thought of that scene whenever I recall my own inability to move that day on the golf course, and in the days and weeks after. It might sound strange, but being in motion—moving—was always what made me tick. It's what made running so natural to me, those long hours and years of practice you have to put in—and want to put in—to become a champion. It was why, though I missed my family terribly at times, I felt natural in planes crossing oceans or trains traversing America. It was as if there were jets inside me and I felt at home hearing and feeling the gigantic jets of the aircraft, or as if there were whirling metal wheels always turning inside me, and feeling the speeding train wheels under me was like feeling part of myself. I loved to walk, as fast as I could, for the same reason. I hated to sit or to stand still.

Now I wasn't even sitting. I was lying flat on my back, with a couple of the best neurosurgeons in the country telling me I would probably be that way again and again and again if I didn't have major surgery on my spine. A bunch of my discs, after years of what I guess was unnatural strain, had suddenly ripped out of place all at once, doing all kinds of damage.

"Must I have this operation?" I implored the doctors.

"You'll live without it," one of them answered. "But no one can say for sure just how much mobility you'll have. You might even be able to walk frequently without pain."

I told them I wanted time to think about it. I hated surgery—not surgery, really, but being out. You had absolutely no control of yourself. Sure, I flew in planes every week of the year, and you have no control there either. But like I said, I felt at home in a plane. I was moving hundreds of miles an hour. I didn't feel I'd ever die that way. But lying flat on my back unconscious in a hospital. . . .

"I'm going to try to make it on my own," I told them. I left the hospital the next day. There was pain, a lot of pain, but all I cared about was that I could move. I was walking on my own, not completely straight, but a lot closer to the real Jesse Owens than I had been lying in that antiseptic bed the day before.

As my first hour on my feet wore on, I was able to stand up straighter and straighter. *You'll do it*, I said to myself. *You'll do it, Jesse.*

I was able to do it for about fifteen minutes. Then everything went again—worse this time. I hailed a cab somehow, and the driver helped drag me into it. I told him to call Ruth, and we met her at the hospital. A few hours later, the same neurosurgeons were standing before me.

"I want you to cut on me," I said. "But you have to know something. I don't want you to do it halfway. I want to get out of this bed and walk and move like I used to, or I don't want to get out at all." I said it quietly, but they knew that I meant it. Yes, life should be fought for and treasured at any cost, but each of us has a unique identity, too. Mine was somehow tied up with being able to be in motion, to seek physically as well as spiritually. I knew that I couldn't survive without it, and I wanted the doctors to know it.

On May 18, 1965, a knife plunged into my body for the first time in my life since my mother had taken the bump from my chest when I was five years old. Only this time I didn't know it.

I was never so happy as when I came to!

Still, there was one big question left. Was the operation a success? In those days, back surgery wasn't as perfected as in the seventies and even now it's a risk.

I had to lie there for days without moving. Then I could only move ever so gradually, because of all kinds of casts and braces and warnings. Eventually, though, I was up and around, and it was obvious that the operation had worked! I was as good as new. Just to make sure, I went back to golf, a game I'd learned to love, practiced intensely for a few weeks whenever I could get away. Two months after my operation, I won the championship of the public course against men half my age.

I put the trophy right next to my gold medals.

The next night, we had a celebration. All the girls came over for dinner, with their husbands and the four grandchildren that I now had. Ruth had cooked as only she can, with Gloria, Beverly and Marlene helping out, and it was one of the most wonderful evenings of my life—one of those evenings where your life seems completely rich. Once or twice during the evening, only because I was so moved by the closeness we all felt, and because now I was on my feet once again like the Jesse Owens of old, my thoughts turned to my mother and father. I wished they could have been alive somehow to see this, but of course that wasn't possible. I did make a firm mental note to call all my brothers and sisters in the days that followed, and arrange a reunion for the "other" Owens family.

After all the kids had gone and Ruth and I were alone, and the house was cleaned up, we became playful. Maybe we were grandparents, but we weren't too old to act like kids! And when we made love, it was no different. It was just as wonderful as that very first time so many years ago in Cleveland.

"You know, Honey," I whispered to Ruth as we lay there together afterward, "I think the storm is over. I think it's all sunshine from here on in."

She didn't say anything. She was asleep. And what was better proof of her own feeling of peace about our lives?

I rose early the next morning, as I'd always liked to do, with the sun. It was one of those glaringly bright ones, so you had to shield your eyes as you drove. It happens in several parts of the world especially—Dallol in Ethiopia, Death Valley, and the Northern Sahara where Luz was killed—and for some reason it always disturbed me a little. It didn't seem right that the sun could be too bright. Or maybe that morning, it was simply a premonition?

When I arrived at my office, there was an official letter from my government awaiting me. I had received many before, but none like this.

It told me that I was being indicted for evasion of income tax, with a possible penalty of the rest of my life in jail.

I couldn't believe it.

"Beware the awful avalanche!"

CHAPTER FIFTEEN

I've got faults, probably more than most. You know some of them by now, but I'd never cheated anybody in my life, especially not my country.

Actually, it was the same old weakness that got me into the tax trouble: I was moving too fast. Ruth had always made out our returns, but after centering my activities in Chicago, I got in with a bunch of people who gradually took it over. Yet tragically, none of them took care of it and stupidly—that's the only word that fits—I didn't make sure.

For four years, I had filed no income tax return. And the fact that it wasn't deliberate didn't make any difference under the law. I could go to jail. And even if I got lucky one more time and somehow didn't, it would only be on the condition that I could rectify what I'd done. And how could I? My income had been big these last few years. The taxes on it were enormous—and the interest on the taxes. It was 1939 all over again.

Except this time they wouldn't give me fifty years to pay it off.

I didn't *have* fifty years to pay it off. I was fifty-three years old.

I was scared. I haven't really been scared many times in my life—not for myself. This time I was.

I had no father to go to. No mother. And the only other person I trusted like I trusted them, was Ruth. And she was scared, too. Very scared.

I did what I had to do. I found the best lawyer in Chicago, a man with a top rep, but who I also gut-trusted once I sat down with him. He questioned me intensively for several days, then said he'd get back to me, that he wanted to begin preparing my defense. He said it would be tough, very tough, but that we had one thing going for us—that I'd made a mistake, hadn't deliberately cheated, and would be willing to pay it back, somehow.

I went back to work, feeling not like the Earth, but Jupiter, was on my shoulders. Yet I had to keep working, because if by any chance my lawyer and I could pull off a miracle, I'd need all the money I could get together with a show of good faith to start paying back my government. It was a government which had given me the chance to go from Oakville to Cleveland to Berlin to a parade lining the streets of New York.

Only the work wasn't there when I went back to it. Sure, there were some accounts that didn't leave right away. Maybe it took them a few weeks, or even a couple of months. That might be because, though bad news travels fast, it doesn't get everywhere right away. Not that they stopped working with me because of my tax trouble. They had all kinds of other reasons like, "We're restructuring and are declaring a temporary moratorium on this kind of spending." Reasons like that.

Did I blame them? No and yes. No, because I was representing them, and naturally they didn't want to be represented by a man who had been indicted for a crime. But yes, in one way I did blame them. Because what crime was I indicted for—did they know that? Wasn't I innocent until proven guilty, too? Most of all, why didn't they have what it took to tell me straight out why they weren't going to work with me any more?

O.K., I told myself, *it's going to be almost impossible to stay in Chicago again. I'll have to make my living by traveling, giving speeches, instruction, like before.*

Except that, within a few months, there were no places to go, no speeches or instruction to give.

Everyone pulled out. The Boy Scouts were the last to go. They held on as long as they could. The very first one—I received their letter two days after the news of my indictment hit the papers—was the National Conference of Christians and Jews.

I'd never been much of a saver. When the money stopped, and the bills didn't, my bank account canceled out as fast as all my other accounts had.

But at least my court date was coming up soon, so the few hundred dollars above and beyond immediate expenses, which was all that I had left, would last until—

Until, even worse than my great-grandfather, I was put in actual chains?

Until—

Mrs. Jesse Owens went back to work as a maid?

Until—

I couldn't even stand to think the thoughts. I can't stand to write any more of them even now.

But if there were only weeks left, they passed like eternity. My family stuck by me, but they were just about the only ones. Walking out in the streets which I used to love so much became torture. The kids never changed. They yelled my name and waved like always. But the grownups—they were beyond belief.

People I didn't know but who knew Jesse Owens, shunning me.

People who knew me well, looking the other way like they didn't see.

And the phone—the phone that always had to have three buttons on it because so many calls came in at once—became like another piece of soundless furniture. Except for my daughters, and kin, it stopped ringing completely. "Might as well take it out and save the money," I joked grimly to Ruth one evening when we sat home alone, hardly talking to one another. "We can call the girls from the drugstore."

There were no attempts at humor after that. Only a week was left. A week until my day of judgment. All of us know that someday we will die and that when we do, we will be judged. We will either have met the test of life, or not. But because none of us knows when our judgment day will come, we can live with the mistakes we've made—and are making.

But I felt that my judgment day was coming not at the end of life, but within my life, and for the first time, I found something which was almost impossible to live with.

For the first time in my life, I thought of taking my life.

But I couldn't—wouldn't—do it. That one line from the movie *High Noon* kept coming back to me. Gary Cooper, the marshal of a small western town, has sent an insane killer to prison. Now the killer gets out and, with three others, is coming to kill the marshal. The irony is that Cooper is no longer marshal. He was married that very morning and is leaving with his wife to start a family and a store in another part of the state. But he feels that he must stay now and face the killers, and asks the town for help. He is shocked when everyone turns their backs on him, out of either cowardice or short-range self-interest. He will have to meet the four killers alone.

They all also implore him to get out. Because if he's gone, there won't be any trouble. But he feels he must stay. Finally, when the last person he depended upon pulls out, the marshal begins to walk toward the stables. He throws a saddle on a horse. He is thinking of running.

His former deputy has followed him there, walks in, begins to get the horse ready. The marshal tells him not to, that he isn't going to ride out. "But you were going to a minute ago," the deputy shouts.

"I was tired," the marshal answers. "A man thinks a lotta things when he's tired. But I can't do it."

As that final week turned into days—five, four, three—I became unbelievably tired, not only in my body, but in that deeper way. But I couldn't give in. Ever.

Yet I knew, though there were only three nights and two days left, that I couldn't face this without help. But who could help me?

Doctors? As James Dickey said, "They can save your life, but they cannot make your life worth saving." The doctors of the mind were no different. They might save your sanity, but not your soul.

Ruth had tried. She had tried as hard as any human being could. But she needed help as much as I did.

For it was my soul that needed saving. Then I knew where I must go.

It happened as I was passing one of those little storefront churches on the south side of Chicago. I suddenly knew that only God could give me help. I went in. I didn't notice the denomination, and what did it matter? Wasn't He everywhere where human beings were seeking Him?

The little church was empty.

I would be alone there with my God.

I dropped to my knees. I closed my eyes.

And then . . . then . . . I knew a terror so frightening that I had never in my most abysmal nightmares imagined such horror could exist.

Bleeding in Oakville . . . owing $114,000 with no way to pay it back . . . losing my parents . . . even . . .

yes, even being humiliated before the world and about to go to jail—
Those things became nothing next to this.
I was shaking, gasping. Was I dying? For the first time in my life, I didn't care. I truly didn't.
For this was a terror worse than death.

This was the peasant's last Good-night,
A voice replied far up the height,
Excelsior!

CHAPTER SIXTEEN

I couldn't pray.

I . . . couldn't . . . pray.

After more than twenty years of traveling the globe to speak to literally millions upon millions of people, I couldn't say a word.

Nor was it because I was praying wordlessly. I simply . . . no longer . . . knew how to pray. . . .

I fled home, in a panic. Ruth had left a note: She was out shopping. The panic grew inside me. It wasn't hysteria, but something cold, suffocating, overwhelming. I had to do something.

I went to the medicine cabinet, and took the pills the doctor had given me for my stomach. The bottle was still half-full, because I'd gotten better without having to complete the prescription. It called for three a day, six hours apart. Even then, they had the effect of making me drowsy. I took three at once. I knew that was safe, but I also knew it might knock me out.

It did. Within fifteen minutes, instead of pacing, I was sitting in my big black leather chair in the den, my body feeling like it weighed a ton. I'll go lie down, I said to myself. But I never got out of the chair. Eyelids of cement closed, blocking out everything in the world. . . .

I dreamed the worst nightmare I'd ever had. I was bleeding . . . bleeding to death . . . I'd been bleeding for days . . . weeks . . . and now I was growing too weak to even scream out . . . couldn't do anything about it . . . could only lie there . . . the blood pouring out of me—

Yet it wasn't pouring out of me . . . I was bleeding . . . but there was no blood on me . . . it was impossible but true . . . I knew I was bleeding . . . but there was no sign of blood . . . how could it be—

I struggled for the answer, but was too weak to think . . . I had so little blood left now . . . so little . . . the last of my lifeblood was hemorrhaging out of me . . . without a single drop showing on my skin . . . how . . . how could it be?

Save me, Daddy! I screamed soundlessly, trying to awaken, not to die. *Pray for me, Daddy—pray with me—I have so little blood left—*

Yet I couldn't pray. I couldn't. It was the only way to awaken, to live, to save myself . . . but I couldn't.

I'm dying . . . I'm dying, was my only thought. I knew I was sleeping, but somehow I couldn't awaken. I was dying. Dying—

I awoke!

Thank God I'm awake, I said to myself. I said it, but I didn't feel it. The sleep was over, but the nightmare was true. I was dying. I was bleeding to death.

Suddenly, I understood the entire nightmare.

It wasn't my body that was bleeding to death, as it had been fifty-three years before in Oakville, Alabama.

It was my spirit that was bleeding to death.

At break of day as heavenward
The pious monks of St. Bernard
Uttered the oft-repeated prayer . . . .

CHAPTER SEVENTEEN

I panicked again—more than ever. I looked at the clock.

Only minutes had passed. I hadn't really been asleep.

I tried to rise from the chair. Couldn't. Couldn't open my eyes again. Now, the pills were truly taking effect. Or was I sleeping and dreaming this? I'll never know. If that's what it was, I sank deeper into it, all the way, all the way back. I was in Oakville bleeding . . . in Berlin jumping . . . at my mother's funeral . . . pulling Ruth's pigtails in fifth grade . . . at my father's bedside when he was dying . . . *Don't give in, Daddy . . . don't give in to it*—

He turned his eyes, but not his head. J.C., was all he said. He closed his eyes. I felt fear as I'd never known grip my own heart like a vise. It was that hour before dawn, that hour when it's blackest, when I realized I was alone with him for the first time.

He opened his eyes. "I'm goin' . . . with your momma . . . now . . . J.C. . . ." he whispered.

No Daddy, you can't.

His lips moved ever so slightly in what might have been a smile. Or maybe he was going to say something. But he didn't.

Please, Daddy, please. Stay with me. Stay with me awhile longer, at least. Please—

His eyes answered.

He was going to die. He was ready to die, and there was nothing I could do to change it.

Daddy, I pleaded. *I don't even know how to pray without you. Tell me how to pray, Daddy. Like that time we did in Oakville. When you saved my life. How did we pray then? How? Tell me how, please tell me how, Daddy!*

I could see him straining—and I didn't want him to, but I wanted him to tell me—oh, how I wanted him to tell me—and then, finally—

The dream kept coming back to my father's deathbed. It was as if it was really happening—and aren't the things that happen inside you more real at times than anything you can see or touch or hear?

But this time . . . he didn't die at that moment. He strained even harder with all the fiber which had brought him through the deadly Alabama fields that had killed Joe Steppart and so many others, that had brought us all from those fields with him, and he choked out those final few words which had been haunting me for more than twenty years—words that only had been unknowable sounds—

I awoke!

And this time, I was truly awake. The luminescent clock on the den table to the right of me read ten to eight. It had been three-thirty in the afternoon when I'd sat down in that chair. The room was dark. Night had fallen. The day was gone. Yet a slight illumination shone from the end of the hall. The kitchen, where Ruth was preparing dinner for me?

There'd be no dinner for me tonight. For now I knew.

I was bleeding to death inside, my soul was bleeding to death, and no doctor, no person on earth, could save me.

Only God could save me.

I had to pray to God to save me. And like the Olympics, I would have to give it all I had.

There was only one place I could do that.

There was only one place I had ever done it.

I grabbed a jacket, rushed into the kitchen, kissed Ruth and told her that I had no time to explain, but that I would be back tomorrow, in time for my trial. Then I rushed out of the apartment, taking the stairs three or four at a time, threw open the door to my car and turned on the ignition almost in one motion. Thirty-five minutes later I was at O'Hare Airport, writing out a check for a round-trip flight which left me with about $30 to my name. Less than two hours after that, I was in the air.

Heading toward Oakville.

A voice cried through the startled air,
Excelsior!

CHAPTER EIGHTEEN

Except that there was no Oakville any more.

Sharecropping was long gone and, with its demise the world around it had virtually vanished. There was no more Oakville, not on the map, anyway.

I didn't need any maps. Seeking was what I'd always loved doing best. It was only when I had run from my searches that my problems had come.

I transferred in Memphis, got off the plane in Huntsville, waited an hour until the bus came that would eventually get me to Decatur. Then, as I had so many times in my life, I began walking toward the Oakville that no longer was.

When you've walked as much as I have, or run, or jumped, in your life, you can tell within a handful of yards when you've gone a mile. And after I'd gone the nine miles between Decatur and what was Oakville, I paused and looked around. It was all different. I searched for landmarks. There weren't any.

Buildings blocked out what had been the land and, where there was open land, it was different. I looked for trees—Oakville had been named because it had so many oaks. But none of the few which remained looked the same.

With a burst of speed, I ran to one in the distance, running my hands madly around it once I got there, looking for initials that Sylvester or Quincy or I might have carved. Nothing.

My eyes darted to a rise in the landscape even farther off. Was it the rockpile where my parents had talked? I raced toward it, but the rocks seemed to fall away with the horizon, further away, and then were gone. It had only been an illusion.

Is my mind playing tricks on me? I asked myself, scared. *Could I be—could I be losing my mind?*

I felt the bleeding coming faster inside myself now. It was as if my entire soul was hemorrhaging!

I know it will sound absolutely insane, but I'm as sure of it to this day as I have ever been about anything: *I was bleeding to death without a single drop of visible blood leaving my body.*

And then, really for the first time in my entire life, I lost control of myself completely. "I must find our little house!" I shrieked out loud. "My daddy will be there—he'll be there waiting for me!"

I began running frantically. This way. That. Was it here? A new factory blocked my way. I ran my hands along one entire wall, feeling, somehow hoping to be able to feel if I was getting closer. *I'll break down this wall to get in,* I swore, *if this is where our house stood.*

No, no, it wasn't here.

It's farther that way—past that rise in the land.

I began running frantically again, the instincts of my spirit—the blood pouring even faster from it now—taking over.

I reached the slope in the land, hurried down the other side, gasping for breath, looking to my left, to my right. It's over that way!

I hurried to my right, but zigzagging as I went, the strangest sensation I had ever known with each passing second pulsing louder and harder within me—the sensation of being physically completely alive, with enough energy, drive, to almost compete in the Olympics, but at the same time my soul empty and dying, dying—

I don't know what I did then, where I went. Trees and clouds, people and buildings blurred before my eyes as, like a blind man, I felt my way toward where our home had been, my hands running across cement and then smooth wood and then rough wood with nails cutting my fingers and then bushes and then nothing.

My hands were grasping in space, and there was nothing to hold on to. No longer was the blood gushing forth inside my soul, because I knew, I knew with the most awful torture a man can ever know and feel that my spirit was almost lifeless.

I dropped down to the soil, my hands digging in, so as not to fall off the earth itself.

From somewhere I heard water—*I think it's*

water—there was just one drop . . . then the next only after the longest time . . . and then finally, after even a longer time, another . . . .

It sounded like that long ago but so familiar dripping from the tiny crack at the top of the big pot where my mother used to boil the meat . . . those rare times of the year . . . it wasn't until the meat was really boiling good at the very end that the bubbles rose high enough to make a drop come out of that crack every so often . . . or it could have been the clothes that momma washed and put out to dry . . . yes, it sounded like the clothes that, even though she wrung them out so hard with her tiny, tensile hands, so you thought there wasn't a drop left, if you went really close, and waited, you could hear drip . . . drip . . . drip . . . from my father's thick work shirt after the longest time . . . or was it right after the first "staying snow" we had, when you were lying snug in your bedding with everyone else all under that same roof and it started to melt and no matter how my daddy and Sylvester had worked on the roof there was that one place in it which went drip . . . drip . . . drip—

"Oh!"

A pain like nothing I'd ever known went through me. I had to cry out loud.

But where had it come from? It was everywhere and it was nowhere. Not from my heart—not my throat—not my gut—

I knew.

The pain wasn't in my body at all.

The drip . . . drip . . . drip . . . the final drops of my soul's blood . . . had stopped.

A traveller, by the faithful hound,
  Half-buried in the snow was found. . . .

CHAPTER NINETEEN

Only my body remained.

I began crawling, as if by some primitive animal magnetic force, across the earth. I felt like the first sea creature must have felt as it left the water for the land. I crawled on. I was looking at trees, buildings, a few people in the distance, but not seeing them. I was hearing the sounds of the world, but unable to listen to them. All I knew was what I felt with my hands and knees against the earth.

I felt the crisp Alabama grass as it always feels in the final days of January.

I felt the soil beneath the grass, cold, but the deeper you dug in, always with a promise of warmth.

I felt the thorny weeds that pierced my fingers and made them bleed the way that my soul no longer could.

I made my way past the grass and the weeds. Just a

few yards further—less than that—I could feel tilled soil and, when I reached to my left and to my right, neat rows of crops . . . of cotton . . . and collards. I closed my eyes to see them better. I heard the wind sweep over the field, and the good smell—all Alabama crops smell good at harvest time—rushed up into my nostrils. I reached out to embrace a stalk of corn between my two open palms. I felt it, its rough husk, with the beginning of a silken tassle at my fingertips. Then I didn't feel it. My two palms were pressed together with nothing in-between. Yet I was no longer in the fields. I was just outside the doorway of our humble house in Oakville. My father was beside me. His palms were pressed together. He was kneeling also.

I heard his voice, crying, "God save him. Jesus, save my son." My soul echoed his prayer.

We were praying together again—this time to save my soul.

And this time . . . I can remember what I said.

But that doesn't matter.

What matters is that, as I knelt there, my soul dying, I said what I said, felt what I felt, with every last drop of blood that was in me and I sensed that there was only one last drop of blood left in my spirit.

Yet I learned in that instant what I'd never truly learned before. I learned something that, once it is revealed to you, can never be unlearned, is always with you.

True prayer means nothing else but giving the final drop of your soul's blood to reach God.

And yet, at the same instant that was revealed to me,

one question and one question only burnt itself into my brain: Was I too late?

I had felt—I swear I had actually felt—that last drop of blood leave me. My soul was empty!

Once, many years before, I had heard of a young athlete who was dying of the most malignant kind of cancer. I flew to the hospital where he lay, and tried to comfort him. I sat beside the bed in which his corpse, down from a strapping 200 pounds to less than 90, still breathed, and at the end—though I didn't know it then—there was this sound from deep within him somewhere. This unholy sound.

I was later told that sound was called "the death rattle."

I waited now . . . to hear the same sound . . . inside my soul.

Still grasping in his hand of ice
That banner with its strange device,
Excelsior!

CHAPTER TWENTY

The death rattle did not come.

I opened my eyes. I was alone, kneeling at the edge of the same unplowed field.

Two things only had changed.

The first were the clouds which before, though big, had billowed lightly above. Now, they were closer, and rain was about to pour from them. It did, but I lifted my face to it, parted my prayerful palms and turned them toward it, feeling the sacred water of the heavens washing over me, cleansing me.

And, inside, I felt a sacred flow. The blood of my soul was pumping once again, pulsing so strongly that it bled out, filling every dark hollow part of my spirit.

It runneth over.

My soul had died.

As it must, for me to be . . .

Born again.

There in the twilight cold and gray,
Lifeless, but beautiful, he lay. . . .

CHAPTER TWENTY-ONE

The following morning I was standing before a different kind of judge.

Ruth and I had said goodbye for a few hours or for years? Would I be saved on earth as my soul was saved?

My lawyer gave the case in favor of me. My government gave the case against me. The judge asked me if I had anything to say before he pronounced the verdict.

I nodded, and stepped forward.

And I prayed.

My prayer was this: "I never tried to cheat anyone in my life, Your Honor—except possibly Jesse Owens—so . . . help . . . me . . . God."

Did the judge know that was a prayer?

Possibly not in his mind, but I think he did in his heart. Because he bent his head for a moment, as I had bent mine, was quiet, and then he said, "Never has a defendant stood before the court but what I haven't taken a look at his record. I hope when I get up above—if I get there—and Saint Peter looks down and finds some of my misdoings, he will at least take a look at the other side of the ledger and see if there isn't something to my credit. I've looked at the credit side of your record. I see enough."

The verdict was that of course I had to pay what I owed, but that I would not even be on probation because my government would trust me. As I left the courthouse that day, I passed a blind man outside, a cup in his hand. I reached in my pocket but had no change. I looked in my wallet. It was empty. I pulled out the section where I kept my driver's license and such things. Wedged between them was a twenty dollar bill I'd always had for emergencies. Also wedged between them was the poem *Excelsior* which Charles Riley had given me thirty-five years before. I had never read it. I read it now. And cried. And decided at that moment that I wanted *you* to read it—as I decided at that moment to write this book, my spiritual autobiography. As for the twenty dollar bill, I put it in the blind man's cup. It was all the money that I had. Now, I had exactly the same as when I came into the world.

With but one infinite difference: *I had found God.*

Though it was more money than I had ever owed before, I paid my debt. Ruth and I built a better life. And I have devoted the majority of my hours since, attempting to inspire others to feel what I feel, know what I now know.

And I paid one other "debt," though I received much more in return. I returned to Berlin, and made good my vow to see Luz Long one more time.

I saw Luz in the face of his son, Karl.

Though taller, Karl was the spitting image of Luz—inside as well as outside. It was as if Luz had come again to see me . . . and it made me know that the spirit of Jesus within Luz, within Karl, within Jesse Owens, within all who know Him, would come again some day upon this earth.

We walked, we talked. We looked at the sights of Berlin together. We went to the place where, in 1936, Luz's name and my own had been inscribed, supposedly for all time, in metal. Our names were still there, but next to them were bullet holes. The bullets which made those holes were no different than the one which struck down my brother, Luz Long. As I threw my arm around him to say goodbye, I silently prayed that no bullet holes would ever be beside the name of Karl Long.

I have tried to do what my father once vowed to do—the hardest thing.

Always keep the faith.

I have found God, but that does not mean I cannot lose Him.

And from the sky serene and far,
A voice fell, like a falling star,
Excelsior!

CHAPTER TWENTY-TWO

This is the chapter I cannot write because, of course, it is the chapter I have not known.

Yet I feel that now I can live it, feel that I can face it.

I am sixty-four years old. I want my life to go on, and on. Or I wouldn't be here. Each new dawn, almost always without giving it a thought, you and I make the one choice on which every other choice is built. We choose to live. And all human lives, on the bottom line, are filled with the same tragedy and triumph, sorrow and joy, loss and love.

But as all of us strive to hold on to the gift, the challenge of life, each of us knows that someday our life on this earth will end. And it is no paradox that if you sincerely want to live, you simultaneously are prepared to die, if you must.

The key is belief.

This is what gives us our greatest, infinite joy. This is what makes the unbearable bearable.

The belief in that which is higher.

So, climb with me upon that summit-less mountain. Go on higher, on, on higher.

Its cliffs are not paved with earthly matters—going higher, higher and higher.

Climb not for the peak you see, but the one concealed to thee.

For, true heaven lies infinitely, above the summit of the mountain.

Higher.

Higher.

Higher.

Amen.